Trogir • Split • Stobrec • Omis

Supetar

SOLTA

BRAC • Bol

Hvar • Starigrad • HVAR

VIS

The Adriatic Sea

Vela Luca • Blato • Korcula • KORCULA

Lastovo

MJET

Dubrovnick

CROATIA

BOSNIA-HERZEGOVINA

DALMATIA

MY MOTHER'S SIDE
A Journey to Dalmatia

Daniel Friedman

CEDAR &
BOXWOOD

Book design and map of Dalmatia by Browning Porter Design

Cover portrait: "Goldie"

Cover photograph of Split by Đanin Tulić – ©iStockphoto.com/ToolX

Author photograph by Philip Beaurline

ISBN 978-1-4507-6565-7
Printed in the United States of America

info@cedarandboxwood.com

Cedar & Boxwood logo
is a registered trademark.

For Nat, who took me there, and Nedjeljko, who took me in.

An Introduction

What more does a man want than an olive tree,
a native land, and woman from his own place?
—Lawrence Durrell, *Prospero's Cell*

———————

On my mother's side I am Dalmatian and
Dalmatia is my land.

Most of us in America come from someplace else, and the overwhelming majority of us have only a dim or imperfect—or entirely impaired—understanding of where in the world we come from, some vast, vague area on an ever-changing map, a place we only knew was once dangerous or destitute and could no longer be counted upon to support our lives. In addition, most of us believe that we are now far advanced from that place of origin, far more evolved than whoever might be left behind. Amnesia sets in fast, connections to the old world are severed, ancient wisdom lost. But the fact remains that, in many instances—if you care to—you can go back in time and space and find your people and learn profound truths from them.

My discovery of a simpler, smaller, accessible life in Dalmatia, among cousins I did not know I had in a village of storybook beauty, took place during a period of malfeasance and collapse in America. The contrast between these two very different worlds—between what I thought we had in America and my newfound family's traditional way of life in southern Europe—thrust itself upon me like characters in a morality tale. Having only just finally extricated myself from an industry that was fast imploding and guilty of nothing short of a complete betrayal of the public trust, I found myself delivered inside an ancient and comprehensible family structure, in the midst of my own tribe, living in the same village, in much the same way, as they had for the past several hundred years. I was lucky to be welcomed into their lives, shocking in its disparity from the world I had just left back home. It was as if a higher power had plucked me one day from America and dropped me the next into Dalmatia, with the intention of opening my eyes and altering my consciousness.

In the process, I found my mother, but I was not searching for her. And I discovered my mother not as she was when she was alive, but as she might have been, or as I had wished I had known her—cleansed of the artifice or ambition of being American. By the date of this accidental connection with my Dalmatian kin, my mother was deceased for two years. The last six or seven years of her life were not of especially high quality, and living on opposite coasts, we saw each other only infrequently, once a year, if that. Our old wounds, over time, had healed, our disputes and unfinished business settled down and long since put to rest. I no longer blamed or disappointed her, we laughed more easily, and expected less from each other.

After decades of work and fatherhood, I was on a genuine quest for myself with this trip to Dalmatia, late in life, a third or fourth try at a fresh beginning, yet another shot at self-discovery and truth seeking. At an age when many just want to hold steady to their course a few more years, or start thinking about downsizing, I wanted to explode everything, throw it all up in the air again, one more time, to see if I had it in me. My life had naturally fallen into installments of ten or twelve-year chapters—and I was ready to commence a bright new volume.

In the city of Split, I found my place, and in the Adriatic Sea I found my mother's womb. I found family who opened their lives to me just at the time in midlife when it was most critical to learn lessons about how to live again. I found large crowds of strangers on city streets and in public squares and cafés with whom I felt utterly relaxed and completely at home. I learned from this family of mine that I come from strong stock, as my mother always used to tell me. I learned that my blood lines will endure, if not in one specific place in America, then certainly in one small village by the sea in Dalmatia. I now know the meaning—and the feeling—of finding one's true ancestral centerpoint. Dalmatia was not only the place for me to be, but also "the place where we would wish ourselves to end our lives," as Anthony Sherley wrote about Corfu in 1601.

"You must have a base," one of my cousins told me, "or you are nothing."

A place of personal truth and connectedness, in the air, the water, and the people. And from that vantage point, I could look back across to my home in America and consider how to begin anew.

At first, immediately after making this intoxicating discovery and recognizing the scope of this gift, I was assailed by doubts about ever returning to America. With my children grown and gone, what good was my old life there? Why would I want to go back? Why could I not take the story of American immigration and reverse it, turn it on end? With Dalmatian grandparents, Croatian citizenship was urged upon me by Croatians who want and need new countrymen. My Italian-American friends sought out their rich Italian lineage and luxuriated in it with pride. I could do the same with my ancestry, my deep blood ties in Dalmatia. I felt comfortable there, I saw my face in the faces that I met, I saw my mother replicated on the streets of Split as a 20 year old, a 30 year old, a 40 year old, and as a grandmother clasping a three-year-old child by the hand.

Most importantly, I learned a lesson about living simply just when the need for this lesson became most critical in the United States.

My journey to Dalmatia came with instructions about hardship and resilience and authenticity and being self-sufficient. For example, what passes for hardship in America and amongst my southern European relations are two entirely distinct classes of trouble. In ex-Yugoslavia, hardship is civil war, mass murder, Srebrenica, occupation by hostile troops, short-range missiles targeting your village for months on end. Learning from them what real hardship looks like, allows me to contend better with what passes for hardship in the United States, and to be more grateful for the safe haven my immigrant grandparents were granted on these shores.

Likewise, there were equally simple lessons to learn about joy. It is a basic human minimum requirement to recognize joy every day, take joy where you find it, for it frequently can be found in small places before your very eyes. Better perspective, an understanding of happiness, and a life of authenticity— everyone in America, if they are able, should take such a trip.

I went in search of my ancestry thinking I would find nothing and discovered a thriving village of cousins the first place I looked. Finding them and knowing them has grounded me like nothing else could, and helped turn my world around.

—Daniel Friedman

One

THE BIG FIRM

It is a beautiful morning in early May, 2008. About fifty of us have gathered at the Greenbrier Hotel for this "rewards trip" to thank us for the good services we have rendered and to bring us up to speed on new products emerging from the Big Firm's prodigious pipeline of dubious investment ideas. Financial advisors are not the world's most handsome species, and this fact is driven home whenever I see a group of us at sales meetings. But what always strikes me first is the noise level. The room is full of contentious brokers shouting at each other.

From the floor to ceiling windows in this Carlton Varney-designed room, I see colorfully dressed golfers walking leisurely towards the pro shop. The West Virginia mountains are vivid green with fresh buds and the purple and white dogwood are in full bloom. To get out and enjoy the place, we must endure hours of presentations, an exacting price. By the end of the day, all I will want is a strong drink.

I take a chair between Roscoe and Bubba, two agreeable brokers I know from previous conferences. In greeting, we roll our eyes at each other, the best we can do. We know from experience that the morning's address will be of no value to our clients. The truth today will also be dangerously skewed. The pressure and volume at these meetings has been ratcheted way up over the years, and the products they are pushing are increasingly incomprehensible. In these final days with the Big Firm, I reckoned, one in ten working in my business was an honorable person who put the interests of his clients above his own. Everyone else was a spinmeister concocting ways to squeeze money from the system.

Today's presenters are three managers in their mid-thirties flown down from the home office to lead the way to sales immortality. They wear dark suits with chalk-stripes, their hair combed back like Reggie in the *Archie* comics. They speak with bludgeoning forcefulness and simplicity, like nightclub bouncers, and conclude their remarks with the phrase, "and wit dat," as in, "thanks for your attention, and wit dat, I pass the mike over to Nick."

The day is devoted to structured products, the Big Firm's investment scheme du jour—Yield Optimization Notes, Notes linked to the performance of stocks like Lehman Brothers, and other arcane investments that don't make the slightest amount of sense to me. Each comes with a ninety-page prospectus in fine print written by a battery of lawyers, and they are presented to us this morning as the brilliant future of the investment world.

Structured products are complicated derivatives that only a handful of people understand. The managers make no effort to hide their lack of expertise about their inner workings. They only skim the surface, waving off serious questions as if we are stupidly missing the point. Ours is not to reason why. We are not to question the Big Firm's great plan. We are the rank and file, the foot soldiers, the sales force.

"Sales! Listen up! This is the future of the business," one of the angry managers is hectoring from the podium, jabbing the air with his fist.

"You are either on board with this or you are not," he threatens.

The ultimatum helps me focus. I am not on board with these insane investments and it is time for me to go.

"Make up your mind," he continues with a left cross against an invisible foe. "You are either on the bus or you are not. It's up to you."

The additional imagery is perfect. I am definitely not on the bus, not with the managers and their products. If baffling derivatives are the future of the Big Firm, then my future lies elsewhere.

I take a deep breath and make the decision to leave. My years with the Big Firm are over. I don't know what the future holds, but it's time to go, past time by a couple of years at least. I'm hoping there is a little life ahead of me. Perhaps I can make another start. Maybe I can achieve happiness. I know I owe it to myself to try.

My last act was to put my name on The List. Seeing my name at the bottom was a shock, like reading my obituary. There I was among friends and people long forgotten, a headstone in the graveyard of the Big Firm. But I was not dead and not sorry to be leaving. Writing my name on The List was a celebration.

The List was created during my years of employment in the Big Firm's office in red-brick Charlottesville, Virginia. It began on a scrap of paper during my first weeks on the job, when it became obvious that employees arrived and departed with astonishing frequency, that someone had to record the staggering failure rate. That's why I started The List. Every time someone left, I added their name to the bottom. The List amazed me as it grew.

The Big Firm's sophisticated ad campaigns were fiction. The List was the truth. On days of sickening market plunges I would remove The List from my desk to update it, copy it onto a larger sheet, or read it aloud to a beleaguered colleague, his necktie askew, slumping in his cubicle. As master of The List I knew it was only a matter of time before my name was added to the bottom.

We had realtors, corporate lawyers, former insurance salesmen, and a multimillion dollar producer who one day lost his mojo, became a changed man, and just walked out. We had twelve recent graduates of the University of Virginia with good haircuts and expensive new wardrobes who were too young to inspire trust among people with money. Four of our rookies failed the Series 7 General Licensing Exam after months of paid test preparation. We hired a man from Shanghai who did not speak English, a personal trainer who got sick and quit, and an elderly gentleman who was terminated for malpractice.

College basketball players, high school history teachers, and retired Marine Corps officers all began with enthusiasm but quickly moved on.

I was moving on, too.

With advice from a friend, I plotted my exit. A good ending was important. I was planning to live out my days in Charlottesville. I would see my former clients and wanted them to be glad, or at least neutral, about running into me at the grocery store. This had to be done right.

First, I selected William, a young broker I trusted, to receive my accounts. Then I listed clients according to their importance to the Big Firm and their sensitivity to my departure. Then I picked up the phone and called everyone to arrange meetings for breakfast, lunch, and drinks before dinner. The first client, after hearing me out, extended his hand with a smile and offered his congratulations.

The day came when the Branch Manager mailed invitations for cocktails at the C&O, one of my favorite Charlottesville restaurants, where gifts were presented, kind words expressed, and all the guests looked happy. Afterwards, a good friend and his glamorous new girlfriend took my wife and I to Tastings, another Charlottesville culinary landmark, where we consumed several bottles of Burgundy and Oregon Pinot Noir. It was a great way to go out—a beautiful summer evening on the last day of August, 2008. The Dow stood near 12,000 after correcting downwards from 14,000 for most of the year.

Friends would later applaud the perfect timing of my departure from the investment business, but I had no foreknowledge of events to come. I simply couldn't take it any longer. Staying on the job another month might have killed me.

Within weeks, the financial world would bear no resemblance to itself. The Big Firm, with sixty-thousand employees and offices and art collections across five continents, would be gutted and broken into shards, sold off to lesser firms with unknown names, its leadership publicly humiliated at angry shareholder forums presided over by the police. And the Greenbrier, the "playground of Presidents," hemorrhaging money and threatening its parent company with bankruptcy, was rescued by a West Virginia coal baron who dreamed of bringing casino gambling to the place.

I wasn't the only one making important changes. My wife was changing, too, and we weren't sure we were moving in the same direction. I was leaving the Big Firm and heading out into the world, and she was staying in Charlottesville. For now, that's all the two of us could be certain about.

Two

THE SAME BLOOD

One week later I am sitting in the sunshine overlooking the Adriatic Sea in a white canvas deck chair on the gravel terrace of the old Hotel Park in Split, Croatia. My tall, inspired, always smiling adult son sits across the green metal table from me pounding away on his laptop. The photographs Nat took that morning show me pale and tired, wrinkled around the eyes, just starting to decompress from departure and arrival, but out of business attire finally and into jeans and a black tee-shirt, and now sporting a week-old beard. We are sitting under the tall palm trees at the Park finishing breakfast. Fifty paces across the street from the hotel is a sandy, crescent-shaped public beach, and even at this early hour, dozens of people are laughing and frolicking in the Adriatic. This is neither the glamorous Croissette in Cannes nor the elegant Place du Casino in Monte Carlo. This beach in Split is much more to my liking. It is a scene out of a grainy, vintage film, one might say a poor man's Riviera, but it is more real, and it teems with life.

Nat and I have the full day ahead of us to explore family history around Split before heading south to Dubrovnik to rendezvous with our Backroads group for our long planned bicycle trip on the Dalmatian islands of Mjet, Korcula, Hvar, and Brac. I have no idea what this day will bring, no idea if there are any remaining members of the Plosnic family in Stobrec, an ancient fishing village built on a very small, rocky peninsula jutting out into the Adriatic, just five or six kilometers south of where we are sitting, and now part of Split's sprawling, urban conflagration. But I intend to knock on some doors. Setting aside only part of one day for this search, it strikes me now with force, will narrowly limit our chances for success.

We arrived at the Hotel Park the previous day, driving south from Nat's home in Munich, and upon arrival in Split, late in the afternoon, I got in my trunks, walked across the street, and swam in the Adriatic for the first time in my life. But I felt an overwhelming sense of comfort and belonging, that I had been in these waters before. Among the bathers on the beach I watched a tall, slightly stooped older man tending a small boy, with a craggy face, large hands, and angular, athletic build, who reminded me of my grandfather, and not once before in my lifetime had I seen anyone who reminded me of my Dalmatian grandfather. Standing there waist deep in the Adriatic, perusing this beach panorama among scores of Splicani of all ages, with whom I seemed to share physical characteristics, I began to relax. I did not know it then, but this is the famous Bacvice Beach of Split, and I would return here every day in the weeks of discovery to come.

That evening, Nat and I set out on foot from the Hotel Park, past the city port, past the crowded cafés along Split's newly renovated and quite dazzling waterfront promenade, and wandered into the narrow stone passageways of Diocletian's Palace, what Rebecca West called "cells in a honeycomb." We had dinner in the Venetian central square, where we sat beneath 15th century towers and absorbed the scene among hundreds of locals and tourists strolling and milling about in the heat of the evening.

After breakfast, I explained to the tall, bright-eyed concierge at the Park that I am an American of Croatian descent, that my family originated in the area, and that I was searching for anyone in the nearby village of Stobrec named Plosnic. I had attempted such a search myself from home with Google and had come up with nothing.

This pleasant concierge smiled in response, went to her computer, and quickly printed out for me the page from the Stobrec telephone directory listing the names and addresses of all families named Plosnic in Stobrec. There were ten names and addresses on the list, ten Plosnic households in Stobrec, a village of stone houses with red tile roofs and just 3,000 souls. It was that easy to find them.

The concierge quickly scanned the page. "This is Konstantin Plosnic," she said with familiarity, indicating the name at the bottom. "He is the owner of the Restaurant

Epetium in Stobrec. It's one of the best seafood restaurants in the region," she said with the authority of a concierge long accustomed to making restaurant recommendations. "Start there. They will know everyone in town."

My heart is racing. Walking on air, I bring this page of ancient Plosnic names and addresses out to the sunny terrace and hand it over to Nat. "Let's go," he said, quickly getting to his feet.

My gentle and loving grandmother Paulina Plosnic was born in the village of Stobrec in 1888, the eldest of eight children. She immigrated to Chicago in 1913 where she lived in the boarding house of a cousin from Stobrec, Mara Blazevich, met and was courted by another boarder, her future husband, my grandfather, also a recent Dalmatian immigrant. His name was Jerry Simundza and he was born in the upland village of Bisko. This distinctly American fact bears repeating: my grandmother, born on the Adriatic Sea, left for the south side of Chicago where she met another Dalmatian immigrant from a village not twenty miles distant from her own, and she married him.

Both my Dalmatian grandparents spoke Croatian only throughout their lifetimes, were comfortable with very few rudimentary words in English like hello, OK, and goodbye, despite lives of more than half a century in Chicago. Neither of them owned or drove a car and they did not own a television. They lived in the Croatian neighborhood on the south side of the city along Princeton Avenue in the racially Balkanized Chicago of that epoch, attended the newly founded St. Jerome's

Croatian Catholic Church, shopped in Croatian markets within walking distance of their home, and spoke Croatian among their friends. Their youngest daughter, my mother, and her three siblings, all born in Chicago, grew up speaking Croatian at home and learned English only at school. At the outset of World War I, the population of this Croatian enclave in Chicago numbered 50,000. Chicago's south side was our staging area, an independent city-state with fixed boundaries. The only cross pollination was with nearby communities of recent Italian immigrants, who shared the identical Mediterranean culture and cuisine. My grandfather grew grapes in his Chicago garden and made wine on the back porch. Michael Bilandic, mayor of Chicago in 1976 after the death of Richard J. Daley, was a neighborhood boy and a classmate of my mother's at St. Jerome's School. A more controversial figure, Fast Eddie Vrdolyak, was another local hero to my mother and her kin. That Croatian neighborhood on the south side of Chicago, more populous than the city of Split in 1913, is now a dynamic and prosperous Vietnamese community.

Like most immigrant families, there was no looking back to the old country after our arrival in America. Once my grandparents took root in Chicago, the bonds with Dalmatia began to dissolve. St. Jerome's is still a thriving Catholic church on Princeton Avenue, new Croatian immigrants in far fewer numbers continue to arrive, but the thick southern European texture of that neighborhood was completely lost in one generation. My mother was a beautiful Dalmatian girl with a quasi-Dalmatian, quasi-American identity—whatever suited her mood at the time—but I was 100% American, a mongrel with a Dalmatian Catholic mother and a freewheeling, street-smart Jewish father.

I loved and felt close to my Dalmatian grandparents and keenly felt their love of me, but I was awkward after a certain age with them because our relationship was limited to nonverbal gestures, however affectionate the intent. They had no English and no one required me to learn Croatian beyond a handful of words and phrases. For a young American boy, English was the language of the new world, of television and radio, Croatian the strange and clumsy tongue of a dim past. I did not especially like the crowded old neighborhood on the south side, the long drive down there in the car from the North Shore where we lived, and had no friends there or activities.

So the connection with my grandmother's world faded fast. Stobrec, Split, and life in Dalmatia became remote and foreign to me. The stories I was told about my family of fishermen in Stobrec and the beautiful songs they sang as they sailed out to sea at night on lantern-decked boats had as much application to my life in the Chicago suburbs as a fairy tale.

As if to mark that disassociation from Croatia and the great forward progress in their new American model, so distinct from that of their parents, but so strange to hear told now, my mother and her sister, my Aunt Dorothy, both with fluent Croatian language skills, visited the then-Yugoslavia, traveled to Split, purchased wooden trinkets and artifacts from shops in Diocletian's Palace still selling identical souvenirs today, and made the short excursion down the road south to Stobrec.

But in Stobrec, birthplace of their mother, they did not bother to look anyone up. They traveled in the worldly guise or sophisticated posture of rich American tourists, a superior breed. They went to Stobrec, walked and explored the village, and did not look to see if any of our family remained. This anecdote, as my own story unfolded, staggered me. They went back to their ancestral home, as my mother called Stobrec, and did not look for their ancestors.

How to explain this?

Status.

By the date of that visit, my mother and her sister had moved way up the economic ladder and did not want to be brought back down. The Croatians who journeyed to America were bold adventurers who crossed the seas and made new lives, if not for themselves, then for their children. They looked upon those who remained in the old country with disinterest or disdain. The modern, split-level home that my mother and father built on the North Shore of Chicago in 1959, with its echos of Mies van der Rohe and Frank Lloyd Wright, had no equal anywhere in the Yugoslavia of that period. In those days, the American Dream worked as advertised. We moved from Dalmatia to Chicago's immigrant south side to the affluent suburbs of the North Shore in two generations. We went forward without fear, and we created wealth and a great new nation. To my mother and Dorothy, the Dalmatians of Stobrec were backward peasants by comparison. We were richer and better. Any shabby cousin encountered in his stone hovel in Stobrec could only be an embarrassment. That's why my mother and her sister looked for no one when they visited Stobrec in 1966.

What they did not know, and I was to learn, is that the village is full of our relatives.

Dorothy is now almost 90, still mentally sharp, and lives in a Chicago nursing home not far from Lincoln Park. After the death of my mother, she remains the last of that generation that transitioned between the old and new worlds. So I called her in the summer of 2008 and told her I was going to Dalmatia with my son. I knew she would be interested.

A few days after that telephone conversation a surprise express mail package arrived from her at my home in Charlottesville. Dorothy had sent me all the Plosnic family documents in her possession, plus a nine-page letter she had written outlining family history and our story of immigration as best she recalled it passed down to her. She was now entrusting these birth, baptism, marriage, and citizenship documents to me, she said, because "I am on the way out, and the history of our family must never be forgotten." All these old church certificates and government documents were carefully preserved and in excellent condition.

The most critical document Dorothy included was the original birth certificate of my grandmother Paulina Plosnic, exquisitely handwritten with elegant flourishes in black ink on good paper, complete with the Stobrec municipal seal, dated October 21, 1888.

With these documents in hand, Nat drove me down the coast road to Stobrec, all of fifteen minutes.

Without Nat's urging I would not be on this road. Without him I would never have conceived of such a trip. I would have found on my own ten middle-aged objections not to go. But after years at the Big Firm I knew I needed a serious detox. I needed time away and new sight lines, and Nat might have thought that my health depended on it. Perhaps I was beginning to look like the financial type I was. So, months earlier, when he asked me to take a bike trip with him I did not need to be asked twice. I looked at the Dalmatian coast trip offered by Backroads, the outfitter from Berkeley, and mentioned it to Nat, along with the notion of an ancillary ancestor hunt. His immediate response: "Let's do it." Then, in a moment of ecstasy, days after the life-changing sales meeting at the Greenbrier, I blurted out to my assistant at the Big Firm that I had just signed up for a bike trip in Croatia and that I'll be out of the office at least a month, perhaps longer. She raised her eyebrows and put a hand on one hip. "Let me understand this," she said. "You will be out of the office for a month?" Brokers never leave the office for a month. It appears I had made two decisions at once: my departure date from work and my departure date to embark on the rest of my life.

Fact is, I would have gone anywhere as long as I was going with Nat, the destination didn't matter. The prospect of a couple of weeks with him filled me with joy. At the end of the bike trip Nat was heading back to work. But I had scheduled three more weeks of open ended travel after the ride, with no commitments or reservations anywhere, thinking vaguely I would like to see Berlin, easy to reach from Nat's home in Munich.

We had a history of travel together, just the two of us, father and son, sometimes under not too shabby circumstances, and this trip was the latest installment. During the years I worked in France, I took him with me on my travels as frequently as I could. When he was twelve we had dinner at Taillevent in Paris where the distinguished Jean-Claude Vrinat fawned over him. We dined at Le Grand Véfour in the Palais-Royal and Le Train Bleu in the Gare de Lyon. Down in Collonges-au-Mont-d'Or, the great Paul Bocuse, a veritable symbol of France, wrapped Nat up in a bear hug. At the Bas Bréau in Barbizon we were kept awake by a strenuous couple in the next room noisily making love, and we laughed out loud at the merriment. As a teenager, Nat met me in London and we flew to Gibraltar and onto Casablanca where we rented a battered but roadworthy Peugeot sedan and ill-advisedly drove ourselves across Morocco from Essaouira to Marrakech, Rabat, Meknes, and Fez, and lived to tell about it. These travels were some of the great highlights of my fatherhood.

As Nat hit his stride in software he turned the tables and started taking me places. Just after his twenty-second birthday, I watched him give a talk at the Jacob Javits Center in Manhattan attended by a crowd of technology investors where I found myself seated next to Mary Meeker, the celebrity securities analyst, who was furiously scribbling notes as he spoke. I visited him in Boston routinely and sat in on meetings as his company grew. I followed him to India where he was the keynote speaker at a technical university in Bangalore, where

I was besieged by dozens of intense young men foisting their business plans upon me, certain I was a VC.

I was his cheerleader but at some point he started cheerleading me. Not sure what I did to deserve such a kid. When you put that much love into a child, you do it because that child is precious to you, and because you know that child will need all of your love to step boldly and happily into a world that sometimes does not give a shit, not with the expectation that your love will be returned. I fueled Nat with *Kubla Khan*, *Oxymandius*, *Fire and Ice*, *Dover Beach*, *Anecdote of the Jar*, and all twelve books of Plato's *Republic*, and now he was fueling me back.

Leave the Big Firm? I asked him for advice, months before departing

"Just do it."

Take off for Croatia?

"Let's go!"

Pedal up that ginormous hill?

"Great going, dad, you're almost there."

We were almost there indeed.

The deep turquoise sea is calm and flat that utterly brilliant morning we pull off the highway into Stobrec. Along the road we pass a large billboard advertising the Restaurant Epetium, our destination, owned by Konstantin Plosnic, the man I hope to meet.

At the very entrance to the village off the highway I have a shock of recognition. In the pine forest along the sea is a campground and I have visited this place before. Nat stops and pulls over. I camped here with Nat's mother in 1974 when we were students on our way to Dubrovnik in the old red Volvo. We were just passing through. We had pitched our tent among these pines and ate grilled fish in the campground restaurant on the beach littered with spiny black sea urchins (which made swimming impossible).

A lovely, smiling woman in peasant dress and a colorful headscarf worn in traditional manner sat at the campground bar that night, just across the room but a world away from me. She had the faultless bronze skin, white teeth, straight brown hair, and upright posture of the Dalmatian race and she was a dead ringer for my grandmother. I would not have known how to begin to say hello. But I knew then in 1974 that I belonged there and that woman was a part of who I am.

Without knowing it, thirty four years ago, I slept in a tent on the shore of my grandmother's village. The image of that beautiful woman at the campground bar had stayed with me. I felt I was among my people and I knew I had to return. This was that day. An hour earlier I expected absolutely nothing from this all-too-brief excursion. Now my heart was pounding with hope and excitement.

Like Split, Stobrec is more than two thousand years old and made of white stone that shimmers in the September sunshine. It has a natural crescent-shaped harbor, like many villages along the Adriatic, with small marina and beach. The old town and village church occupy high ground on the rocky peninsula to the north, and the luxurious Meridien Lav Hotel is just a kilometer or two to the south. Cheap-looking, litter-strewn, low-rise apartments built during the Communist era sprawl away from the sea. The old town consists entirely of stone houses, perhaps no more than one hundred of them, with red tile roofs, Mediterranean architecture at its most pure. Anyone who has explored Provence or coastal Italy or southern Spain or Greece has seen all this before in similar dress, except the children playing football on the narrow stone streets of Dalmatia are speaking and shouting in Croatian. Split is known for its blue collar moxie and urban pulse, a scaled down Naples or Marseille, but my grandmother's Stobrec is small, desultory, and off the beaten track. It possesses a tourism office staffed during the high season, a Konzum grocery store, two public bocce courts, and four or five cafés facing the Adriatic each with three or four clients sitting by the window, mostly older men, smoking, playing cards, or lost in reverie. Plus, of course, the Restaurant Epetium, its culinary high point.

We park in the center of the palm-fringed Stobrec waterfront and get out of the car. Just above us, mounted on the side of a building, is another billboard for the family restaurant with an arrow indicating the way up the hill into the old town. With Dorothy's documents in hand and my son at my back, I start walking briskly in that direction, my breath quickly shortening to match my uptempo. I am striding up the hill now on the street called Mornarska, the "Street of the Fishermen," where six of the ten Plosnic households reside, according to the village telephone directory, at numbers 1, 3, 4, 7, 27, and 41, stone houses all, some attached, some freestanding, and all perhaps no more than one hundred meters apart. At the very crest of the hill, where the stone street narrows to the width of an oxcart and where the tall white houses block out the relentless sun, I see the arched entryway to the Restaurant Epetium, set in a doorway and down a flight of steps, a cavern or cellar door effect.

I am not thinking and have not stopped to calm myself or gather any speech or coherent words of introduction. I have not dressed for the occasion. I am in the same black tee-shirt and jeans from breakfast, have not shaved for a week, and I am knocking on the locked door of a restaurant looking for people I have never met, who have no clue that I exist, or am arriving at that moment on their doorstep to claim them as my own. The door is locked; the restaurant is dark. I knock again with the dim hope of rousing someone from the rear, but Nat tells me firmly, dad, the place is closed for lunch. It says so right there. Open only at dinner. It's 11 A.M. and we are supposed to be 200 kilometers down the coast in Dubrovnik that night. I am not sure how we are going to get to Dubrovnik and I don't know where we are going to sleep. I knock again—loudly.

Suddenly, from across the street so narrow I could nearly reach my hands to the other side, from the top floor of a handsome tall stone house, the neighbor woman has flung open her lime green wooden shutters, responding to the urgency of my pounding, and says something down to us, in sketchy English, about the restaurant being closed. I am simultaneously disheartened and encouraged by her appearance because she looks, even from across the street and up three floors, oddly familiar.

"Where is Mr. Plosnic?" I shout at her, sounding deranged, I'm sure.

"Upstairs," she shouts back, pointing to the apartment door directly above the restaurant. She is indicating a more contemporary entrance, a plate glass door with drawn white curtains.

I march up this flight of stairs to the family apartment, hear stirring through an open curtained window, and knock again, this time with more care.

I am standing with my son before a house in Stobrec, village of my grandmother, lost in time and far away, forsaken by my family for 100 years.

"Who is it?" a woman asks from within, a melodic voice, not unfriendly.

"Is Mr. Plosnic home?" Strange, speaking the long lost family name in this routine context.

"Yes. Just a moment," she says, in fine, unaccented English.

And the front door of this house in Stobrec swings open wide and my mother stands framed in the wooden doorway, my mother if she were forty years old again, my beautiful young mother, and she is smiling at me with a tilt of her head and a wrinkle of curiosity in her eye. She stands relaxed and confident, smiles naturally and openly, a hint of the coquette, a younger, happier version of my mother, my mother reborn carefree.

This is my mother if she never left Dalmatia, never saw Chicago, and never lived in the United States.

This is, in fact, Tatiana Plosnic, my exquisite cousin, and the documented proof I carry with me of my lineage and connection to her suddenly becomes superfluous or redundant. I need no proof or paperwork to validate my link to this person. She is mine, I am hers; I am of her, she is of my mother. I have hit the mother lode, the grand slam to win the World Series, the genealogical jackpot. I have found them the first place I looked, my true and real family. I have found a beautiful blond female cousin in a sunny stone house on the Adriatic Sea in Dalmatia and I cannot take my eyes off her.

This is a lot to heap on someone who has just opened her front door to two strangers, one collected and quietly observant, the other agitated and overcome by emotion, with eyes as wide as saucers.

"Come in," she says, stepping back into the foyer with a quick sweep of her hand, a gesture that immediately recalls my Aunt Dorothy. Now she's both my mother and my aunt, the light and the dark, and I have not yet stepped inside her house. She is of medium height, she is wearing a white top and white pants, and she has an attractive, trim figure. Her excellent English is an enormous relief.

"You look like my mother."

She laughs out loud, bending forward slightly at the waist. We are standing in the entry hall to a spacious home. Perhaps that's way too strong a beginning.

"You look just like my aunt."

She is not alarmed or put off by any of this—our unannounced arrival at her home, my appearance, and my bizarre opening statements. Good.

She's actually laughing and has a look on her face like: "Well, OK. Go on." She is wearing a necklace with the letters of her name spelled out in gold—TATIANA.

I try to back up and start from the beginning.

"My grandmother was born in Stobrec," I say, spilling out my envelop of documents onto her hall table—the birth certificate, U.S. citizenship certificates of both grandparents, photographs of my grandmother Paulina and I at Christmas in 1960.

"I am in Croatia with my son for a bicycle trip on the islands starting tomorrow from Dubrovnik. I had no idea there were any Plosnics left here"—a colossally misinformed remark. "The concierge at the Hotel Park printed this page for me this morning from the phone directory and told me to start my search with you because your restaurant is well-regarded and that you would know everyone in the area."

Tatiana nods.

"And you look exactly like my mother. You are beautiful." She laughs again, enjoying the utter inanity of my proclamations.

Her nose, the shape and spacing of her Slavic eyes, her skin tone, the curl and color of her hair, the very shape of her face, are all my mother. But she has an unguarded quality—a spark—I never saw in my mother.

"Are you related to these other Plosnics?"

Handing over to her the printout of the Stobrec phone directory, she reads out loud: "Ante Plosnic—yes; Bartal Plosnic—yes; Jere Plosnic—yes; Stipan, Matko, yes, yes, all of them, yes. We are all one family."

All one family.

Tatiana holds my grandmother's birth certificate, and reads from it: "Paulina Plosnic," she murmurs.

Hit with this wave, standing there in her hall, I start to blink back the tears. I think, this is not great form in a country that places a high value on male strength and want to compose myself. I have been in her house three minutes and I'm already crying. Tatiana fixes me with a look of compassion and puts her hand on my arm. "Yes, of course, of course, I understand. It's natural. We are the same blood."

The same blood.

She has a beauty mark high on her cheek like Marilyn Monroe or Cindy Crawford in the identical place my mother had a beauty mark.

At this moment, Tatiana's father walks into this entry hall from an adjacent room where he had been dressing or organizing himself. This is Konstantin, the pater familias, head of the house, white haired and bronze skinned, very upright and fit. His deep-set eyes are clear, kind and intelligent. He is seventy-six years old and Tatiana is his baby, the youngest of his three children. His hands, strong and calloused, are disproportionately large for his body and his most distinctive physical feature. His hands make my hands look pale and soft in comparison, like they have been doing nothing more strenuous than office work. Konstantin is no stranger to physical labor. He has the hands of a stone mason. Weeks later, when examining photographs of the two of us together, I see that I have his nose, his mouth, his eyes, and his easy smile. I hope I am as happy and healthy when I'm seventy-six. He is the kind of big-hearted man any boy would be lucky to have as a father, uncle, or guide through life. He is wearing leather sandals, olive colored shorts, and a navy blue polo shirt open at the neck.

Tatiana explains to her father what she has learned from us and Konstantin picks up the handwritten birth certificate and slowly reads from it the names of Paulina's parents, "Ivan and Ivanic," as if attempting to retrieve some long forgotten fact. The purpose of our visit is coming into focus for him. He picks up the citizenship documents and the family photographs I've brought and looks carefully at each. Then he places the documents back on the table and takes a step towards me and begins to examine my face with great intensity from very close range. He is not shy about it. His scent is that of my long dead Dalmatian grandfather.

Then, standing there in his foyer, this kind old man takes my face between his large, powerful hands, holding me still like a block of wood or stone, and turns my head from side to side to study me from every angle, and then suddenly he's kissing me on my forehead and on both cheeks, holding, gripping me, embracing me in his arms and exclaiming, "Mama Mia! Mama Mia! Mama Mia!"

The philosopher king of Stobrec has validated me as one of his own.

Gripping me by the arm, Konstantin takes me and leads us in a growing procession through the house to the big sunny rooftop terrace at the rear. It's clear this is where the family spends much of its time in good weather. There is a large outdoor dining table with eight chairs upholstered in blue fabric under a capacious blue and white striped awning, and a panoramic view from above of the surrounding rooftops of red tile, the crescent beach of Stobrec, and the stark Mosor Mountains just outside the village. We have been joined by Rudy and Anna, Tatiana's younger children. Konstantin sits at the head of the table.

This first gathering of extended family would be my introduction to the most gracious and naturally well-mannered of any people I have ever known and ever will know.

Breathless, and shocked by the turn of events, I try to explain to him who I am and how I got here. Tatiana translates my hurried narrative to her father, and based on his range of facial expressions, she does an effective job. I tell the story of Paulina's immigration and life in Chicago. I describe her Croatian neighborhood and its insularity, how she met her Dalmatian husband from Bisko in the boarding house of her cousin Mara Blazevich, and how my mother's generation and mine gradually lost all touch with our Dalmatian origins.

Konstantin, searching for connection, speaks to me in a seamless blend of German and Italian. Considering my deficiencies in both languages, it might have been better had he stuck with Croatian.

Tatiana then matter-of-factly tells Nat and I that her family has lived in Stobrec for 800 years. She calls Stobrec "the village of origin." The magnitude of her remarks do not immediately sink in. Konstantin says that this large house has been the family home for at least 150 years, and that he started the restaurant 42 years ago, constructing all of it with his "ten fingers," holding those massive hands in the air with a smile. He is proud of Epetium. It's his creation.

Konstantin brings a book out to the terrace which he offers me as a gift—a newly published *History of Stobrec*, written by his cousin Matko Plosnic who lives just down the street—which records that in the first official census of the village, taken in 1725, Stobrec had seventy four total residents, eight named Plosnic and nine named Blazevich, all my blood relatives. In 1725, twenty five per cent of the village of Stobrec was family to me.

The village of origin.

————⟫•⟪————

Konstantin walks around the table now with tears in his eyes, squeezes me by the shoulders in his vice-like grip, and kisses me repeatedly on the forehead. "Mama mia," he exclaims. These words I understand. His embrace is overwhelming to me. My own father, who adored me, never held me like this.

Tatiana lives in this large white stone house above the family restaurant with her father and mother, her husband, and their three children. Tatiana's older brother Darko has taken over from his father in recent years and now runs the restaurant. Darko and his family live outside the village, a short distance down the coast. Tatiana, who trained as a classical violinist, works in Epetium most nights. Tatiana's mother has been bedridden for many years after a series of strokes. Her care, which is demanding and exhausting, falls entirely to Tatiana and her father, with help from friends and relatives in the village. Stobrec was founded by the Greeks around 300 B.C. The original Greek name for this settlement on its peninsula in the Adriatic Sea was "Epetium," the name my family took for their restaurant.

In the hours ahead, cousins and neighbors will trickle in to take a look at the pair of curious newcomers who washed up on Konstantin's front door. The woman from the tall stone house across the street is a Plosnic herself. Tatiana's lovely seventeen year old daughter, Zora, looking like any American girl her age, and strikingly like my older daughter Peachie, comes home from school for lunch. A friend of Konstantin's arrives to hear my story. He asks if he may make photocopies of my documents in order to construct a family tree. He says that between documents stored in the Split archives and the Stobrec church records, this should be easy to accomplish. People young and old drift in and out, introducing themselves with a smile.

Copious amounts of food and wine start to arrive, large platters of aged prosciutto and chunks of country cheese, fresh grilled eggplant and grilled white peppers all soaked in fresh olive oil, baskets of homemade bread, and bottles of rosé and red wine made by Konstantin from his vineyard. The luscious olive oil he produces from his grove of olive trees. This is an exquisite meal. Seven year old Anna, with her long brown hair, offers Nat and I some of her Mentos.

Konstantin is proud of the wine. He calls it "nature"— completely organic, not an ounce of spray. He drops a cube of ice in my glass, as is customary in Dalmatia, and the rosé exceeds for freshness and color and fruitiness anything in my experience from Bandol, the Camargue, or the southern Rhone. Maybe the setting helps make it special.

"We are a simple people," Tatiana is telling me. "But we have each other."

Konstantin invites Nat and I to stay with them.

"And you can stay as long as you wish, but you have to work," he says with mock seriousness. Nicest offer I've had in a long time. I can picture myself helping harvest his grapes.

I ask if anyone has ever made the return to Stobrec from America or elsewhere as I am doing today, the journey of immigration in reverse.

"No, never," he replies, smiling, without hesitation. No one has ever made the return visit from America.

But he knows all about Chicago. He has a cousin and childhood friend who left the village for Chicago sixty years ago and who never returned. "I invited him many times but he never came," Konstantin says with genuine sadness.

"It's much more beautiful here than in Chicago," I say to them.

We can't cover a hundred years over lunch as much as we try.

I ask about the Yugoslav war of the 1990's and its effect upon Stobrec, not a subject seized upon with much enthusiasm. The war is an open wound. The family friend was a soldier in the war and has a back injury to show for it. He points to the hillsides above Stobrec where shells fell short of their intended target, the Meridien Lav Hotel.

Tatiana tells me that this friend is a real estate expert and that Konstantin consults with him from time to time because her father owns "many lands."

I heartily commend the food and wine. "No one eats this well in Chicago," I say. Unless you are Charlie Trotter, Chicago's most famous chef.

Konstantin replies with an old joke, translated with humor by Tatiana: "American food," he tells me, "has no taste. American flowers have no scent. And American women have no passion." Tatiana watches my reaction to this and we laugh uproariously. I don't attempt to describe the wonders of my local Whole Foods back in Charlottesville.

No one I meet in all of Dalmatia is under any illusions about the quality of life in the United States. No one expresses any envy of my life in America, and no one expresses any curiosity about it. They already know everything about America they care to know.

The wine has me up and out of my chair toasting our gene pool and DNA. Konstantin and I clink glasses, arms around each other, smiling for the 100th photograph Nat had taken that day.

Suddenly it's past 3 P.M. and I'm mortified. We have taken up their entire day. Nat and I still have to check out of the hotel and somehow get down to Dubrovnik.

"When are you coming back?" Tatiana asks with warmth, a tone suggesting she'd welcome our return.

"The bicycle trip ends in Split next Friday."

"Come to the restaurant for dinner."

"We will!"

Back at the Hotel Park on Bacvice Beach the pleasant concierge who unlocked the mystery of my family history in Dalmatia was still on duty.

"How did it go?" she asks.

I tell her and thank her, and want to stay and talk, but now we're in a rush to hit the road.

"Wonderful," she tells me.

"You can come back and be the mayor of Stobrec," she says.

This stops me in my tracks. The mayor of Stobrec. What a thought. What a crazy idea.

I did not expect the forecast to change so quickly in my favor. Only one week earlier I was a dying animal trying to extricate myself from a job that was killing me. In seven days I exchanged the company of the belligerent managers for the enchanted world of my cousin, the stunning Tatiana Plosnic.

Three

ISLANDS IN THE SEA

I am American, Chicago born....
– Saul Bellow, *The Adventures of Augie March*

The face of Tatiana is with me like an icon everyday on the bike trip. Tatiana's beautiful Slavic face is superimposed above the road ahead; at the crest of each hill is her easy smile, and the cheerful melody of her voice is my companion, the background music to my exertions in the profound heat of the bright Dalmatian mornings. So too is the image of my grandmother Paulina in her dark braids swimming in the sea at Stobrec as a little girl, my eyes welling up with tears in the front room of their house, Dorothy's documents spread out on their table, the look of comprehension coming over the face of Konstantin, his wholehearted acceptance of me, his physical scent that brought my grandfather back to life.

On my mother's side I am Dalmatian and Dalmatia is my land.

Dalmatia is distinct from Croatia. Dalmatia is the mother of Croatia. Dalmatia is the Mediterranean, the rocky, sunny Adriatic shore, and its archipelago, its broken mosaic of islands in the sea, all at one time a province of the Roman empire. Dalmatians are a pure Mediterranean race and a sun drenched tribe, descendants of the Illyrians, the Roman legionnaires, and the original Greek settlers, but their own nation separate and distinct from Italy and Greece. Croatia is the mountain hinterland, a dark and eastern breed apart.

True civilization begins where olives and garlic grow.

It's nice to know where you come from.

Did my grandmother regret leaving the beauty and connectedness of Stobrec for the south side of Chicago? She must have regretted it, at the very first blast of a Chicago winter. Did she hope to return to Dalmatia to live or to visit? What was Stobrec like in 1913? How dire were its circumstances that this young woman, born in the nineteenth century, made a perilous journey from the village of her birth across strange seas, leaving her known world? How could the endless bounty of the Adriatic Sea have failed them? What ship did she sail on for America? Did she depart from the port of Split? Ellis Island has no record of her arrival. Where did she first reach American soil? By what means did she travel from the east coast to Chicago? Paulina's life in Chicago from 1913 through two world wars and the Great Depression was no picnic. My grandparents' Chicago bungalow was seized by the bank in 1932. What will Dorothy make of all this?

After the death of Marshall Tito, Yugoslavia's great World War II hero, the fall of the Berlin Wall, and the collapse of the Soviet Union, the former Yugoslavia was split into six separate nations based upon ancient ethnic, religious, racial, and tribal loyalties—Croatia, Serbia, Slovenia, Bosnia and Herzegovina, Macedonia, and Montenegro. In 2008, a seventh country was created, Kosovo. But seven nations from one still may not be sufficient. Dalmatia, my relatives believe in their heart—even with a population just under one million—is its own republic and the engine of the new Croatia. The upland Croatians, with their dark hair and central European features, have been moving in waves to coastal Dalmatia for the same reason people from the northeast of the U.S. wish to relocate to the beach in South Carolina. It's a universal desire, for those who have the means, to live in a sunny climate near the sea, in a green economy dominated by travel and leisure. Dalmatian cities on the Adriatic like Split, Trogir, and Zadar are booming with new residents and the established families are not at all happy about it. Even scenic little Stobrec by the sea has grown by a quarter. The original families hold social power. Relations or friendships between the classes of old and new are unthinkable.

"They come, they want to be our friends," Tatiana says shaking her head. "They want to be like us. But they are not like us in any way. They do not look the same, speak the same, or think the same." Odd to see this snobbish and exclusive side of my Stobrec relatives. What would my mother have made of this?

Stone ruins, abandoned houses, island vistas, the sun, the sea air, and the scent of lavender, vineyards without end, fields of figs and olive trees, the ubiquitous carob, fishing boats and pleasure craft, the heaps of garbage and rusting vehicles.

I am an American, Chicago born, the product of four immigrant grandparents, but first and foremost a Jew in the eyes of my well-intentioned Waspy friends back home in Virginia. Jew is a recognized brand in America, unlike, say, Dalmatian, and I must read Jew to them, and forgive them their confusion. Fine distinctions are futile, even with my best of friends.

My life among the Wasps was to be identified as a Jew, and subtly isolated in that way, but never to be fully or meaningfully accepted by the Jews themselves. Real Jews know that Judaism is matrilineal by ancient law, and the real Jews would no more include me in their tribe, with my Dalmatian Catholic mother, than any other goyim without total conversion to the faith, and conversion to Judaism is no easy matter. A rabbi on the North Shore known for his charisma and intelligence called me "an assimilate" when I was a teenager trying to find myself, not exactly an embracing welcome, and a comment which marked my exclusion. I loved my father and my father loved me, but I felt pushed aside by the Jewish elders. I am an American mongrel, I always told myself in private moments, and took strength from that and loved America for its mongrel spirit and its mongrel strength.

My boy Nat, leading me up these hills, is in equal parts English, French, Dalmatian, and The Pale of Settlement, but he too finds himself identified from time to time as the Big

Jew on the basis of his name, slipped the secret handshake, recipient of the knowing nod. His engagement to be married to a beautiful and brilliant Bavarian girl was reported by *Valleywag*, a Silicon Valley gossip site, with the headline: "Nat Friedman to Make Shiksa Girlfriend an Honest Woman." We roared with laughter about it but it becomes absurd. I told Nat that, only twenty-five percent Jewish, Heinrich Himmler would still have included him in the roundup for Dachau. By sheer coincidence, Nat and I both reread *Night* by Elie Weisel the week before the bike trip.

After the brief but intense plunge bath into the deep end of our Dalmatian gene pool, Nat and I will now spend a week exclusively with rich Americans cycling along the islands in the sea. It's quite a contrast.

We leave Nat's car—a VW Toureg Nat christened "Mr. Bluey"—parked halfway up the sidewalk behind the Hotel Park and ride the comfortable public bus filled with young tourists five hours down the coast road to Dubrovnik, happy not to have made this harrowing, cliff-hugging drive ourselves, soberly assessing the scale of the mountains, passing through an assiduous and less-than-friendly Bosnian border checkpoint, arriving late in the evening, and finding a nice but grossly overpriced room on the outskirts of town at the Hotel Neptune. The next morning we assemble at 9 A.M. at the lovely Hilton Imperial in central Dubrovnik and meet our group of fellow travelers for the first time.

Nat and I have never taken a Backroads bicycle trip and before today I had never seen myself as an active traveler. A round of golf riding around in a cart with another overweight golfer as my companion was as much exercise as I got. For years, my vacations consisted of cigars and cognac out on the terrace at sunset after a bottle of Bordeaux with dinner. In fact, neither of us had ever traveled anywhere with a group of any sort and did not know what to expect from group travel, and were not especially sanguine about it. We were in Dalmatia, we were going to ride, we had each other, that was more than enough.

The group members we meet that morning are all outgoing people. There is a female cardiologist and a female radiologist, longtime friends traveling together from Portland, Maine, who prove to be experienced and outstanding cyclists, three female attorneys from Manhattan who work in the securities industry, four lawyers from Greenwich, Connecticut, two tax lawyers married to each other with their own accounting firm in Philadelphia, and a lawyer for a very well-known Palo Alto venture capital outfit and his sweet and athletic wife. The couple from Philadelphia are on their eleventh Backroads trip; the couple from Palo Alto are on their ninth. Everyone else is new to Backroads and new to this world of luxury bike trips.

Fifteen guests total, five men, ten women, eleven lawyers, and when Nat and I are included, thirteen Jews—a random sampling of affluent Americans that speaks volumes about the service economy, office work, and, I think to myself, a society hamstrung by litigation. It does not surprise me to learn that Maggie, one of the attractive and bright New York lawyers, manages the human resources division for the Big Firm. Maggie and her friends, the two other lawyers from Manhattan, are the very picture of American success: Ivy-educated, living in doorman-buildings on the upper east side with their adorable small white dogs, wearing big Rolex wristwatches encrusted with precious stones, and holding senior positions in the compliance departments at Merrill-Lynch and Goldman-Sachs. All four of the Connecticut lawyers, a man and three women, provide counsel for Gargantuan, the famous Greenwich-based hedge fund, which made billions in recent years. Like me, these seven highly compensated financial services attorneys look tired and pale, but at least they are setting out on a sun-filled vacation.

Our entire group is instantly sociable and easily interacts throughout the week save for the hedge fund attorneys who speak in code to one another and stick entirely to themselves. Everyone else becomes friends. Everyone has a Blackberry or an iPhone. Most of the guests are in their early 40's to early 50's.

Mike and Mary, the couple from Palo Alto, become fast friends with me and Nat. Mike immediately reminds me of my smart younger brother, another legal bulldog who takes enormous pleasure in the give-and-take of healthy argument.

"Are you a lawyer?" I ask him.

"Is it that obvious?" Mike replies, a little subdued about being so quickly found out.

"Either that or a librarian from the Bodleian at Oxford. But your appetite for arguing and winning points that are not being contested made me guess you were a lawyer," I tell him.

To his credit, Mike laughs. He has my brother's good sense of humor, too.

"I apologize," I tell him. "You remind me of my brother. That's how I talk to him."

Mike asks about my cycling experience.

The mountains on the horizon have turned me humble—and a little frightened.

"None," I say. "The only thing tougher for me than going uphill is going downhill. And there do not appear to be too many level spots here in Dalmatia."

Backroads provides two "group leaders" for this trip and they prove to be magnificent: Riccardo, a young and handsome former professional racer from Italy, and Pamela, a long-legged ex-can-can dancer with the Crazy Horse in Paris for six years, a unique skill set for someone leading a bike trip. These two alone are worth the considerable price of admission—they are tireless, charming, helpful, considerate, and great company. The seven single women on the trip all adore the dashing Riccardo, and all the old men have a crush on the lovely Pamela.

Our magnificent vessel for the week, which carries us, our gear, and our fancy new bikes from island to island, is the "Dalmatian Goddess," a wooden, twin-masted, 100-foot motor-sailer, complete with a captain, cook, and a historian-political commentator-general hand rolled into one named Niko—all great guys. The stately Dalmatian Goddess draws a crowd of gawkers wherever we pull into port. From time to time during our travels the captain finds an exquisite sheltered cove, where we leap from the rigging into the warm and clear Adriatic waters.

Finally, we have little Eva, a dark-haired, olive-skinned, 19-year-old tourism student from Dubrovnik who drives one of the heavily laden support vehicles full of food and drink. Backroads does not disappoint on any score. It is one well-oiled machine. Six employees to fifteen guests is a ratio that guarantees great service, and this team does not miss a beat. We sail in the morning, ride as much as we want during the day, and sleep in an excellent island hotel each evening.

We board the Dalmatian Goddess in the busy port of Dubrovnik and set sail for Mjet. It is already 95 degrees and I have a large lump in my throat as I examine the topography on the approaching shore. Mjet is a cycling challenge unlike any I have faced. I have been riding for a year or so and started training in earnest when Nat and I signed up for the trip. I was finally logging fifty to sixty miles a week in the beautiful green hills to the west of Charlottesville. But this is a far more stark and difficult landscape. First day's warm-up ride: twenty-eight miles with 2,600 feet of climb.

We arrive at the ferry landing on the island of Mjet. Riccardo fits us on our shiny titanium bikes and off we go, fifteen riders, up that first hill towards Sobra.

A couple of hours of numbing effort later, I have a great sense of accomplishment as I complete the ride and enter the lovely harbor at Pomena. True, I finish last, fifteenth out of fifteen, overtaken by everyone by the second or third climb, including the pasty-faced hedge funders talking in shorthand as they pedaled past. But I did it. Nat stuck with me, going by, coming back, checking on me as if he were my collie. It was "challenging"—biker's code for miserable—and hot. Mike was waiting for me, conspicuously drinking a beer in a café in a nonchalant pose with a look on his face like: "Oh, finally, there you are. Kicked your ass."

But I wasn't having any of that. Besides, Mike could not have been there more than fifteen minutes.

The least inhabited of the islands we would visit, Mjet is also the most green, with its entire western flank dominated by one of the deepest pine forests and one of the few pristine national parks in all Croatia. We had the roads virtually to ourselves. Local legend has it that Odysseus, returning home from the Trojan Wars, shipwrecked on Mjet and stayed seven years, seduced by the sea goddess Calypso.

At the feast on the outdoor terrace overlooking the finely etched harbor that evening at the Hotel Odisej—prosciutto, grilled shrimp, eggplant, and other Dalmatian delicacies— the Backroads guests are talking among themselves about the magnificent inland lakes we passed and the twelfth century monastery built upon an island, all of which I somehow missed.

The photographs Nat took of me that day show a focused, but only marginally conditioned cyclist, pedaling with his head down, marshaling all of his forces, pushing hard just to transport his torso up hill in the heat, with one mission only: to avoid the ignominy of stopping to get off and catch my breath because the climb was too steep and grueling, admitting on that very first ride that I was not up to the task. This shame I successfully averted. Nat's second batch of photographs show a very proud and exhilarated looking guy with a wide grin that night on the terrace at dinner.

The riding would get more difficult before it became easier. The next morning, after sailing to the brilliant green and vineyard covered island of Korcula, we had a relatively flat twelve mile ride along the beach into the exquisite walled city of Korcula, a magnificent mini-Dubrovnik, then after lunch, a twenty-six-mile ride with a six-mile, eight-degree uphill climb, one of the toughest of the trip. I was quickly learning that if we had a big downhill run into a town, we would have a climb of corresponding difficulty on the way out. At lunch at a pizza joint in Korcula's main square in the company of the two physicians from Portland, Nat asks if I object if he ride on ahead at his natural pace. Not wishing to hold him back, I encourage him to do so, with the result that I ride alone during the tough afternoon leg and don't see another rider until arriving that evening at the Hotel Feral in Brna on Korcula's south coast. I am so exhausted I cannot locate the hotel front door, and enter, in my confusion, through a basement-level service entrance. Again, I am the last rider to cross the finish line.

I am late for my appointment with the massage therapist in the Hotel Feral spa which Riccardo arranged for me when I mentioned neck discomfort after the first day's ride. The therapist turns out to be a young local woman who greets me with a look of impatience and disdain. For the hour I am on my stomach she lectures stridently about unwelcome foreigners on Korcula buying up houses, land, factories, and entire islands across the Adriatic, paying off corrupt Croatian officials to secure illegal building permits, the mess in Sarajevo, and the "wild" Serbs and their terroristic military tactics. She drowns out my sincere attempts to convince her that tourism has an upside and that the diverse global village is an idea worth considering. I leave the spa of the Hotel Feral agitated and disturbed, the worst 100 kuna I've ever spent.

Korcula is an altogether different experience from the tranquil natural area of Mjet, and indeed, each of the islands has its distinct character and flavor. Korcula is large, twenty-nine miles long by four miles wide. It has a significant population of nearly 20,000, an ancient civilization dating from the fourth century B.C., a four hundred year vassal-state relationship with Venice most evident in the architecture of the handsome city of Korcula, and several beautiful, bustling villages like Blato and Vera Luka. There is also a texture of age-old insularity about its isolated country villages of gray stone that can make it feel forbidding and closed to outsiders. Korcula has its share of fig trees and olive groves, but it is covered from end to end with vineyards of a wild, rusticated sort, abundant, lush, sprawling and unmanicured, not immaculate or gussied-up for the tourists like the postcard perfect vineyards of Napa and Bordeaux. Korcula is one of the wine centers of Dalmatia, and indeed the entire Mediterranean region. Its vineyards are among the oldest in all of Europe. Between its small family operations and important wine cooperatives, the island produces more than two million liters per year. Korcula is best known for its delicious, high-alcohol red wines, Plavac, Plavac Mali, and Dingac.

At dinner at the Feral on Korcula, the mannerly New York lawyers inquire enviously about my massage and I tell them it was one part massage nine parts irate political harangue. Interesting anecdotes from the long spectacular afternoon ride across the mountainous spine of Korcula are exchanged over an excellent meal. Mike tells us that while riding through one of the villages, a boy who looked about twelve-years-old attempted to ram a broom handle into the spokes of his front wheel while the kid's mother looked on impassively from their front garden. Odd to select Mike for an assault because he's as large as a linebacker. The Philadelphia lawyers riding behind Mike witnessed and verified this story, and later were themselves targeted by a couple of rock throwing ten-year-olds. On this particular day at least, Korcula is not a happy island. Or perhaps our group had the bad luck to encounter the only four or five people on Korcula not yet entirely on board with the declared mission of Croatia to grow its economy in the direction of the art of hospitality.

Early the next morning we say goodbye to the Hotel Feral, a fine facility in an exquisite natural setting, where the rooms numbered in the two hundreds are located curiously on the first floor, and rooms numbered in the three hundreds are found on the second floor, and pedal up and out of Brna, eleven miles west to Blato, where we get caught in a soaking downpour right in front of a café-ice cream shop on Blato's busy main thoroughfare. Riccardo is standing casually by with his support vehicle, the New York lawyers are sitting warm and comfortably chatting in the back, so it's easy for me to throw in the towel and call it a day. I hand my bike over to Riccardo, hop in, and ride along with them in the van the rest of the way to Vera Luka. Pamela has already collected the Greenwich crew in her van. I quickly discover, however, that all the other riders have impressively stuck it out and rode through the rain, and in forty-five minutes the sun is out again, shining brilliantly. It has become clear that there is at least a moderately competitive element to these luxury bike trips, and I'm distinguishing myself as one of the rear guard.

Nat and I have now spent more time together and in closer proximity since he was a boy living at home in high school. He has been incredibly considerate, allowing me choice of beds, control of the thermostat and television remote, and the time for lights out. At least three times a day I am astounded at his thoughtfulness and my good fortune to have him as a traveling companion.

But something is bothering him. It turns out that Nat is now feeling guilty about leaving me behind on the rides. He and the two Portland physicians are by far the strongest riders in the group, and the three of them are stretching it out, flying around the hills, miles ahead of everyone else, and riding the "long option" on every daily route.

"Dad, I feel like I'm abandoning you," he tells me with a straight face. "I feel like Rabbi Eliahou's son," he says, utterly deadpan.

This is a crazy reference to one of the great themes of Elie Weisel's *Night*—betrayal of the father—and completely, wackily, out of context.

There is no humor in *Night*, yet we both laugh insanely, aware that laughter is probably sacrilegious. Elie Weisel is a hallowed figure—recipient of the Noble Peace Prize. No one ever, in the history of this book, has joked about it.

In Weisel's account, the kindly Rabbi Eliahou and his son were brutally run through a blizzard and the darkness of night for forty miles. Any of the concentration camp prisoners who stops running is instantly executed by the S.S. guards. The rabbi's son, in his desperation, runs on ahead, hoping to distance himself from his ailing father when it appears that the Rabbi is too frail to survive. The young narrator of *Night* witnesses this terrible event and vows forever to be a good son and to watch carefully over his own father.

"Nat, this is not *Night*," I say. "This is a Backroads trip. A more accurate comparison is two guys playing golf together. I may not be able to break 90, but that doesn't mean you can't shoot par."

"Thanks, Dad."

Besides, I do not intend to be the slowest rider in the group much longer.

We reboard the regal Dalmatian Goddess now bound for the island of Hvar, a three hour sail. Hvar is the jewel of the islands, the glamor spot of the Adriatic, a glimmer of what all Dalmatia wishes to become, a magnet for beautiful young people and "the hippest upmarket destination in the Adriatic, a favorite of yachting Mediterranean cognoscenti, those looking beyond Mykonos and Capri," according to a recent issue of *Departures*. Hvar town graced the cover of *Condé Nast Traveler*, which called the island "Europe's New Riviera."

On board, I tell Mike the obvious, that I'm struggling, that I need a better strategy for tackling the big climbs. He makes a suggestion that transforms my trip: "Sing *One Hundred Bottles of Beer on the Wall*."

This simple tactic, along with a quickly improving level of fitness and emerging pride, start to energize me.

One Hundred Bottles of Beer on the Wall sung with enthusiasm two or three times in succession and I am at the top of the largest hill in Dalmatia. I ride on Hvar as fast and as strongly as I ever have in my life. I quickly catch and pass the Philadelphia lawyers; I make Mike and Mary look like they are pedaling through wet concrete; I even pass one of the super fit Portland physicians. I am victorious. I am shouting at the top of my lungs the few phrases in Croatian I recall from my Chicago childhood as I race along the stone walls and the rosemary and lavender covered hills of Hvar.

"Sto novaga?" I am stupidly bellowing at a landscape of stone barns and cottages, figs and olive trees, as I fly along ("What's new?").

"Nista novaga!" I reply ("Nothing is new"). "Nista! Nista!" ("Nothing! Nothing!"). I am a lunatic propelled by adrenalin and endorphins, the native son returned to his ancestral ground.

We stop in the gorgeous seaside village of Stari Grad for lunch after a thirty-mile ride, I am one of the first to arrive, and I am strutting around like I own the place. I decide to sit in a café in the central square and order a glass of white wine over which I can look bored when Mike pulls up.

All the big Dalmatian islands, including sophisticated Hvar, are surprisingly marred by enormous dumps of trash and wrecked vehicles and the most beautiful islands roads can be strewn with litter, with no visible cleanup effort underway or citizen or government initiative in place to deal with these eyesores. At a thoughtless and undiplomatic moment, I mention these unsightly dumps to the local woman seated next to me, who quickly becomes defensive and says that the dumps have always been there, and besides, America has its own problems. I agree. I add that Hvar is like paradise and it could be improved if the dumps were eliminated. She agrees. We go back to the wine.

Hvar has tourism infrastructure and an uncloistered, unfettered 21st century feeling about it. I could be in Mediterranean France. All the rock-throwing troglodytes are back on Korcula. In their place we encounter hundreds of other Lycra-clad cyclists, dozens of Germans and Italians on expensive racers, several other American bike groups, squadrons of French cyclists tearing down the hills on amazing, lightning fast tandems, and scores of others all over the island on mountain bikes. We are staying on Hvar for two nights at the Hotel Podstine, a pleasant walk along the sea from the ancient town of Hvar where Nat and I go for dinner.

It's September 14th, and there are serious rumblings that reach us from back home that all is not well on Wall Street.

Since leaving the Big Firm, I have been in celebration mode and made a conscious effort to detach and insulate myself from all English language news sources, all matters financial, and all things American. I am completely caught up now with Tatiana, Konstantin, the stunning discovery of my large family in Stobrec, life in the Mediterranean, and my only recurring thoughts surround Konstantin's friend and his ability to learn anything concrete about our ancestral connection from Paulina's birth certificate. This is all I really care about at the moment. Nat also helps me decide, after considering all the options available, that I will stay in Split at the conclusion of the bike trip, find an inexpensive place to stay for the remaining few weeks, really explore Dalmatia, soak in my gene pool, and get to know my newfound family to the extent that they are willing and interested in letting me get to know them. Nat will return to Munich on his own, and he is really unfazed about making the long drive back home to Germany by himself.

At dinner, Nat and I sit with the New York lawyers, who have spent the late afternoon at the beach down below the Hotel Podstine in lounge chairs pounding away on their Blackberries sending emails back and forth with worried colleagues at the office. Maggie, the director of the Big Firm, shakes her head at me, looking a little grim. "You left at the right time, Dan," she says.

The next morning, we wake up to the news that Lehman Brothers has filed for bankruptcy and the Dow is in free-fall. No one knows where this is going, but everyone knows there's a big problem. Maggie and her friends are speculating amongst themselves in hushed tones about additional layoffs in their already depleted units at work. For certain, Lehman Brothers going bankrupt means that the structured product based on the value of Lehman stock, foisted on us at the life-changing sales conference as the future of the industry and sold to mom and pop clients by the Big Firm, was now worth zero, a complete loss. The only way to lose money faster was in Las Vegas.

The bad news from abroad elicits a bifurcated response among those at the Hotel Podstine on Hvar. The Americans are shaken and freaked out and the Croatians don't give a shit. I am seeing the wisdom of belonging to the second group.

That evening at cocktails, Backroads has organized a guest speaker to discuss history and contemporary issues in Croatia, and to answer all the naive and America-centric questions that come up from our group. The speaker's name is Mara, she has pure Italian-Dalmatian features—bronzed skin, thick, straight, fair hair, and a Ciceronian nose. She introduces herself to us by saying: "I live here on Hvar where I belong with my family." During the Yugoslavia war she worked as a translator for British journalists whom she escorted to the front lines, and she speaks barely above a whisper, still traumatized by the terrible events she witnessed during that brutal war. She is thoughtful, well-traveled, and university educated, owns a seasonal restaurant on a nearby island accessible only by small boat, and spends the winters very quietly, she says, fishing and making olive oil. Her comments about Serbia, nationalism, the Catholic church, possible NATO membership, inclusion in the European Union, and all the other hair-trigger issues in the Balkans are as positive as they can be given her experience of life. She says she does not remember a time she could not swim, and that operating a boat comes naturally to all islanders. The Adriatic is still clean, she tells us, "hvala bogu" ("thank God"), but not as pristine as it once was. When she reopens her restaurant each spring the beachfront cleanup takes a month, with debris on the beach from as far away as Albania.

Mara is typical of many people I would meet in Dalmatia who possessed refinement, discerning intelligence, and a way with words, and who worked in what many Americans would consider a menial occupation. The attendant at the laundromat in Split I frequented had a bright look in her eyes, smiled with charm, and spoke English flawlessly. Niko, our handyman on board the Dalmatian Goddess, could lecture with erudition on any subject contemporary or historic. The men I met had an easy going, one day at a time approach, staying optimistic, not worrying about accumulating too much money, and always working hard in the high summer season. "If you need 100 kuna for the day," Niko told me, "and you make it, that's enough."

Tell that to the hedge funders on the bike trip and they will laugh in your face.

Mara studied in Italy and lived in the Netherlands and knows what she has here on Hvar. "The Mediterranean quality of life, the fish, the fresh grown vegetables, my olive oil, my uncle's wine." No one looks frightened on the streets of Dalmatia. Everyone has enough. The people are friendly and open. No one is flipping out over the fall of financial assets and decline of the wealth effect. And, more miraculous, there are only two or three psychiatrists in the entire city of Split. Everyone I met had spent considerable time out of the country, has seen the world, and would not trade anything for what they have at home.

The next day AIG asks for and receives an $85 billion government bailout, and the hemorrhage in stocks continue.

As the American, then global, debacle unfolds, my heart connection to Dalmatia grows. Perhaps I am stuck with America, a permanent exile from my Dalmatian village of origin, but maybe I am not. Perhaps Dalmatia offers a solution for me, an example of a way out, a clue to a new beginning. Maybe Dalmatia offers a remedy, something I can bring back to America and make work there. Not everyone wants to give up their credit cards, their club memberships, and their two-acre lots in the subdivision to catch tuna and sardines in the Adriatic, to move back to their ancestral villages in Italy or Greece or Scotland, or to farm the land on a homestead in Vermont or Tennessee. But it's legitimate to seek an alternative to our gut-wrenching cycles of fear, our financial house of cards, and our national priorities and obsessions that grow more weird with every passing season.

Perhaps not every American kid should be encouraged to grow up to be a lawyer. Lawyers, possibly, do not lead particularly happy professional lives. Perhaps a country with too many lawyers is not a good thing and it's conceivable that is the state at which we have arrived. Perhaps not every ambitious graduate should aspire to an MBA or financial engineering as the highest calling. It may be that happiness and comfort are not totally dependent upon income. Maybe there are better tools for making a living than a phone with which to threaten, berate, or sell. All brokers and lawyers need is a license and a phone, and they can go on selling and threatening for a lifetime. For me, those values have run their course. It's over for me.

To their credit, the Backroads guests pull themselves up and out of the bad news and make the mighty effort not to discuss what's going on back home. Everyone honestly looks relieved to be out of the direct line of fire for the moment. The mess will still be there for them when they return. Right now we are amidst the jasmine, boxwood and olive groves of Hvar and it's time to ride.

I get stronger with every ride in the days ahead and it appears everyone else is getting stronger too, staying longer in the saddle, riding further, and climbing more with less complaint. I'm getting a little of that bronzed Dalmatian look myself. Now everyone has ruddy cheeks and looks healthier, even a little bit taut. We all have broken through. It's an amazing experience to get in shape while on vacation. It helps that the temperature has dropped. In a single windy day it has gone from summer to fall.

The last two days are spent on Brac, an island of brilliant white stone and magical forests of old cypress. We stay in the unforgettable village of Pucisca, in the stunning Hotel Palaca Deskovic owned by the charming, chain-smoking Ruzica

Deskovic, whose beautiful paintings decorate her fifteenth century palace hotel. This is a fitting final scene to conclude a memorable holiday with the son I adore. Brac has some of the most beautiful beaches in the Adriatic, including the famous beach at Bol, and it is one of the largest and most mountainous of all 1,200 Dalmatian islands. Nat would ascend to the very crest of Vidova Gora, the highest peak in the entire Adriatic. He shows me the panoramic video of him celebrating at the top.

Like Hvar, it is easy to fantasize about a life on Brac, a cottage with a garden and a view of the sea, a beautiful beach just down the hill, a simple place in the sunshine to stay and swim and eat good food several months a year. Indeed, island life in the Adriatic captured the fancy of Rebecca West too, who considered purchasing property here before ruling it out. "Could we buy some land?" she wrote in *Black Lamb and Grey Falcon* near the outset of World War II. "Could we build a villa? It would be a folly. To get there from London would take two nights and two days by rail and steamer, and I do not suppose that either of us would ever be on easy terms with a language we had learned so late. But the sweet wildness of these bays, and the air rich with sun-baked salt and the scent of scrub, and the view, made this one of the places where the setting for the drama is drama enough."

However, I could get to Brac from the United States in less than twenty-four hours, the flight to Germany, a one-hour connection to Split, and a one-hour ferry crossing. The solid and noble stone houses with their perfect Mediterranean gardens are rife with intrigue and possibility. Brac has an abundance of these well-made villas carved into hillsides, with hidden stone staircases, and architectural curiosities called "bunjes"—conical vaulted stone huts built for storage and protection from the elements. The quarries on Brac that produced the stone for Diocletian's Palace in Split and, some claim, the White House on Pennsylvania Avenue, are still in production, and the amazing white shingles on the roofs of the island homes are massive and thick. How to account for all the gorgeous abandoned houses? Every similar house in the south of France was renovated a generation ago and now costs a million euros and more. These places can be bought for one-fifth the price.

"They build beautiful towns and villages," Rebecca West wrote about the Dalmatians. "I know of no country, not even Italy or Spain, where each house in a group will be placed with such invariable taste and such pleasing results for those who look at it and out of it alike."

But hundreds of the prettiest houses on the islands of Brac, Hvar, and Korcula are empty.

In addition to the genocide, mass murder, crimes against humanity, the war criminals still at large, and at least 150,000 killed, the Yugoslav wars of the 1990's displaced nearly two million refugees. Croatians who lived in Serbia and Bosnia picked up and moved south in a hurry to Croatia; Serbs who lived in Croatia abandoned their homes and returned to Serbia; and Bosnians of all religions and ethnicities fled wherever they could for safety, even turning up in sufficient numbers in

Charlottesville to form their own sizable Bosnian community which endures to this day. Many will never return. That abandoned gem of a home on Brac might well be owned by a Serb who ran for his life and who may or may not one day opt to reclaim his property. Several such homes with questionable title have been offered by unscrupulous agents in recent years and sold to unwitting overseas buyers, who renovate, move in, and are one day visited by the original owners who want their house back. Of course, none of this has deterred large numbers of British and European buyers who dream of a picturesque stone cottage overlooking the Adriatic Sea.

I encounter one such fellow in the bar at the Hotel Palaca Deskovic when I walk downstairs for a drink before dinner, an outgoing German named Manfred who has rented rooms somewhere nearby. "How did you find this place?" he asks me in wonder, as if I were Columbus and he Magellan. "By bicycle," I tell him. The village of Pucisca is an absolute marvel to him. He is in the company of an exotic-looking woman with long lustrous hair and dark flashing eyes, who was beguiling but not forthcoming, withholding herself from our light conversation, so I asked her where she was from.

"Serbia!" she replies with sharp defiance, as if expecting to be assaulted, fixing me with her flashing eyes.

"Cool!"

Maybe she just discovered Londoners occupying her father's former home.

The most exhilarating ride of the Backroads expedition is planned for our last day on Brac. There are several options:

the basic twenty-eight-mile ride with 2,600 feet of elevation gain from Pucisca to Milna, and the full-bore sixty-five-mile option with 6,100 feet of climb. There are also several routes in between. But we all start together that chilly morning and ride out of Pucisca in the direction of Milna. That first climb out of the village is a bear, with hairpin turns and switchbacks on exposed and windy roads with no guardrails. When a bus blows past you are forced to the shoulder with nothing but a little gravel separating you from a big fall into a rocky crevasse. It's very hard work for the first few miles. Then, after reaching the top, we cruise along the ridge lines with smaller up and down hills for many miles until beginning the long, seven-mile final downhill run into Milna. As I pump the brakes down these final hills I promise myself that there is no fucking way that I am riding back out of here. Milna is a busy yachting and fishing center, and beautiful young women are sunbathing nude on the pebble beach in front of the restaurant where we stop for lunch, altogether a memorable venue.

After recuperating at lunch, I ride the shuttle bus above Milna to the top of the hill, then get out and bicycle the rest of the way back to Pucisca, getting lost a couple of times and asking directions from a pair of polite little boys, then finally pulling in front of the Hotel Palaca Deskovic having ridden a total of thirty nine miles for the day, with 2,900 feet of climb, a personal best. My Garmin Edge 705 G.P.S., a going away present from the Big Firm, indicates I have ridden 160 miles over the course of the entire trip. I am proud of myself. Not bad for a broken down stock broker. Nat arrives an hour or so later having ridden the entire sixty-five miles. His Garmin unit tells him he has ridden 120 miles more than his old man during the week. He should be ashamed of himself for leaving the old Rabbi in the dust, I tell him. Big Mike from Palo Alto is the last to get back to the hotel. He has ridden well over fifty miles on the day and is trying to act like it's no big deal, but we applaud him. No falls, no injuries, and only happy faces in our group. Needless to say, a lot of wine from Korcula and local plum brandy is consumed that night in final celebration. It's almost time to return to Split.

Sitting in the pure sunshine of the clear morning I ride on the prow of the Dalmatian Goddess, sailing now to reconnect with my maternal bloodlines, separated by a sea, an ocean, a continent, and 100 years of human turmoil. It's Friday, and tonight we have a date at Epetium. The human settlements along the shore that glisten in the sunshine look so fragile from the sea, as if just tossed and left there by the wind and tide. But we clung to that narrow stony shore, and we thrived there.

"There's Stobrec," I point out to Nat, as we sail along the coast, pointing the direction home.

We cannot have too many loved ones around us in this lifetime, and we will travel any distance to find the place where we are loved.

There is grandeur and ceremony arriving in Split from the sea. Our big wooden boat pulls alongside the pier amidst the bustle of the docks, the tourists gather round to admire our craft, and we disembark and make our goodbyes to each other in the brilliant sunshine of the Dalmatian summer afternoon.

Four

AN OLIVE OIL CENTRIC UNIVERSE

Even with the well-connected Ruzica Deskovic from the Hotel Palaca Deskovic in Brac calling all of her elegant friends in Split on our behalf, there is still not a single hotel room to be found anywhere near the Split city center. There is a yacht race with ships from around the world and an antique auto show in town this weekend, plus all the usual end-of-the-season tourist activities, and the city is completely sold out. She finds us a place for €400 a night several miles outside of town, but Nat suggests we can do better on our own. Dalmatians know they must make hay when the sun shines, and in-season room rates at hotels on the coast are nearly as costly as any in southern France or Italy.

The port of Split where we land is contiguous with the busy city bus station, and vendors of all sorts position themselves to sell Croatian football jerseys and food and drink to the newly arrived, along with "sobes" (guest rooms in private homes). Even the least discriminating traveler can generally judge the quality of the sobe by the dress and comportment of the individual brandishing the handwritten "sobe" sign. For instance, the woman we saw wearing a red tee-shirt at the bus station in Dubrovnik, imprinted with the expression: "Bitch—Just Not Yours," likely does not maintain her sobe to standards that I might find acceptable, but of course I could be wrong about that. Nat and I agree that we would take a sobe for the night only as a last ditch measure. The sobe purveyors who attack people descending from the public buses late at night with a passion bordering on desperation, it may be safe to conclude, are almost certain to be avoided at all costs. These desperate sobe salespeople can be found in bus stations all over Croatia. However, I need a room not just for one night, but a place where I might be comfortable for several weeks, so a sobe is not going to work for me long term. I am hoping for something more livable, a little larger, with a kitchen, maybe even a view of the sea.

We sidestep the sign-wielding lodging entrepreneurs and carry our baggage into a small, semiofficial looking accommodations office next to the port, staffed by another tall, intelligent, multi-lingual Dalmatian woman who, had she been American, would have graduated with honors from Brown or Swarthmore with degrees in comparative religions or mergers and acquisitions.

Although initially I have my doubts about this port-side rental operation, Nat quickly assesses the place and gives me the thumbs up, nodding at me like it's OK to proceed. Nat's probably right; he has been traveling a lot more than I have over the last decade and hasn't been wrong about anything yet.

I tell the young woman that we need a one bedroom apartment that is clean, safe, and centrally located, and within certain price points.

She sizes us up fast, indicates she has such a place, points out its location on a city map, and when I say we are willing to see it, she gets on the phone and calls "the agent," to whom she speaks the only fewest number of words, as if in shorthand. She's off the phone seconds later and says to Nat and I, with the utmost care, as if afraid we are about to bolt: "Please, stay, he will be here in a moment."

While seated in black plastic armchairs in this cramped and dimly lit office, our entire Backroads retinue, all the lawyers and hedge fund managers, our friends looking like the tanned and affluent Americans they are, all walk past and wave so long to us, on their way in an air-conditioned shuttle bus that will take them back to the Split airport. Nat and I have now officially jettisoned ourselves from the Backroads bubble. In Bangalore, Nat and I stayed at the comfortable Oberoi Hotel, and every day Nat urged me to get out of the hotel into the city, to get "out of the bubble." It appears that's what we are doing again here in Split.

The agent arrives in about three minutes and he does not resemble any real estate agent I have ever seen anywhere in the United States. This agent is dressed in the prevailing style of many young and middle-aged Croatian men—like a thug or hit man. It appears that many Croatian men between the ages of 25 and 45 are required to compete in a daily reality television show called "Who looks the toughest?" This fellow was typical: he has a round shaved head, three day's stubble, a gold hoop earring, an unstable, shifty look in his eyes, and all black clothes. He is definitely not the concierge at the Ritz.

The agent introduces himself to Nat and I as Bozo (pronounced "Bo-sho") and he has arrived at this booking office on foot. He explains to us that he does not have the keys to the apartment in question, and that he does not have a car. We will ride in a taxi with him to the place where the keys are located, we will collect the keys, and then we will drive to the apartment, and that he will pay for the taxi himself if we like the apartment or not. Nat agrees with this plan before I can think about it and now the agent is lugging my fifty pound suitcase and heaving it into the trunk of a cab operated by another toughie with shaved head with whom the agent appears to be on familiar footing. In the ride through north Split in search of the keys, Bozo brags about the quality of the apartment we are about to see—"many government officials stay there"—while appraising us up and down from the front seat. I am thinking it's unlikely we are being kidnapped because it's broad daylight, and Nat and I are both large strong men. The agent also says with a smile and a wink that if we like the apartment "we can negotiate the price like a couple of Jews." He says this like he thinks we will find the comment incredibly amusing. Bozo's English is not especially good.

"Did he just say what I thought he said?" Nat turns to me and asks.

"Not really sure, son," I reply.

After retrieving the keys from a building in a congested residential neighborhood, the cab heads south again and then pulls in front of one of the most beautiful little squares in all of Split: Tonciceva Street, just twenty steps off Marmontova, the all marble and brilliant white pedestrian street that leads straight down to the Adriatic, one of the landmark streets of Split's revived city center. The square is packed with cafés, sandwich shops, and designer boutiques, three blocks from Diocletian's Palace, five minutes from Split's massive city market, just up the street from the city's famous and spectacular fish market. Throngs of fashionable people are dining, shopping and lingering all about. Our destination, the apartment building at number 6 Tonciceva, is stucco painted a bright yellow-orange with a red tile roof, and surrounded by a grove of tropical palm trees and other historic, yellow and orange-hued structures. I am far too suspicious of Bozo to take in just how spectacular this is. The fact is, this place is a dream come true. I could stay here a year, or forever.

We ascend a flight of stairs, Bozo gripping our bags, and enter on the right side of the first floor landing to an exquisitely renovated apartment. There's a center hall, a large bright bedroom with French windows overlooking the square, a beautiful new kitchen and dining area, a study with pullout sofa, a luxurious new bathroom, and high ceilings throughout.

The bedroom and study have large flat panel televisions with worldwide satellite, there is cable Internet access, and the entire interior has been painted a cheerful light yellow to match the building's exterior. Plus, there is a large sunny outdoor terrace overlooking the constantly changing scene in the busy square below.

Immediately suspicious, I cannot fathom how a guy like Bozo has obtained access to this apartment. Did he steal the keys? Is the owner out of the country and in the dark about this transaction? There is something wrong here.

In dramatic fashion, Bozo spins on his heels and tells us he wants €100 a night for the place and that he wants to be paid in cash, in advance, for all three weeks, but there is something soft about his presentation, despite his stentorian voice, that make us think this is only his opening volley in the tough negotiations among us Jews. Nat tells him before I can get a word out that since I am staying three weeks, we will offer eighty euros, which Bozo immediately accepts. Eighty euros. I could not stay at home for less than eighty euros. Bozo wants us to accompany him to his cousin's jewelry shop in the old city to complete the transaction, and we follow him out the door, down the stairs, and through the marble honeycomb of old Split. The cousin's jewelry shop is across the street from the municipal tourism office in the center of Diocletian's Palace.

Inside the little shop, Bozo, his tall, dark, unsmiling cousin, Nat and I hammer out an agreement, and it takes some time.

"Bozo," I finally tell him. "You are a prince of the city. That much is clear. But you must recognize that I only met you minutes ago in the Split bus station. One should not be judged too harshly for failing to pay so much cash in advance to someone just met, even someone so obviously charming and well-connected as you. So therefore I will pay five nights cash in advance, and will return here to pay the balance when due, but you must give me a receipt indicating that you have received from me cash payment in advance."

This speech is extremely effective until mentioning the receipt. Bozo's hopeful face and that of his cousin fall flat. They are now crestfallen, full of hopeless consternation, muttering among themselves, planning a retort.

"Of course I need a receipt," I tell them with indignation. "What if some third party appears at the apartment and attempts to throw me out? I must have something to show them as proof I have paid in full."

"Plus, I work for the Big Firm," I lie, handing over a now invalid business card. "The Big Firm requires a receipt from me wherever I travel on official business."

Bozo and his cousin examine the familiar logo on my business card and work through several drafts of a receipt before they write one that is acceptable to all of us. Then I walk down the street to a cash machine and withdraw sufficient kuna to pay them for five nights, thinking this is one of the most rash and stupid things I have ever done.

Nat and I then return the way we came, back to the gorgeous yellow building at number 6 Tonciceva, and start to settle in.

"Dad, this apartment is so cool. It's right in the center of town. You are going to love this place. I wish I could stay with you. Dad, look at this place. Don't you love it? Dad, what's bothering you?"

I still cannot quite come to terms with the disparity between Bozo's personal style and the high quality of the apartment. This cannot be as good as it looks. Something somewhere must be wrong.

"You don't think I am going to be murdered in the middle of the night do you?"

No—but Nat takes several "last photographs" of me in the apartment just in case, out on the balcony, in the staircase, and outside by the front door, as a record of my residence at 6 Tonciceva.

Back now from our island journey, I send a long catch-up email to my wife and daughters. Email was spotty on the islands, and I include all my information here, in the event I am never seen again. Nat sets me up on Skype so I can make phone calls that sound like I'm calling from the bottom of the sea or the space shuttle. If you really want to baffle your newfound Dalmatian relatives, I was to learn, call them using Skype.

So we clean up and dress a little more carefully for dinner. For the first time in a several weeks I put on a blue oxford cloth shirt and a pair of pressed khakis. I shave off my ragged gray beard for the occasion and instantly look ten years younger. Then we start walking across tropical Split in the direction of the handsome Hotel Park to see if Mr. Bluey is where we left him, and indeed he is, half on the street, half up on the sidewalk, side mirrors retracted, without so much as a scratch on his distinctive blue body. I told Tatiana we would arrive at the restaurant at 7:30 and it appears we will be precisely on time. Nat says this is being "Japanese."

On the drive down the coast road to Stobrec in Mr. Bluey, I am anxious and excited again, uncertain what the evening will bring. I am trying to keep my expectations in check. Nat is in another of his Rabbi Eliahou moods. I don't know what potion he has consumed, but he is inspired. He is telling me with authority that we are not related to any of the nice Plosnics in Stobrec, but that in fact research will prove that Bozo and his cousin are our closest relatives in Croatia. Nat cracks up. I am going to miss his company, his warm physical presence, his free-flowing conversation, and I am grateful to him for his love and guidance. We have purchased flowers for Tatiana and candy for Anna and Rudy. Nat looked for Mentos all over Split and had to settle for some sort of Mentos knockoff.

The two of us park again on the seafront of this two thousand year old village and walk up Mornarska Street to Epetium. The restaurant is lit up to greet us this time, with the sounds of voices and music coming from within.

When we enter, Tatiana is standing behind the bar in a simple white dress opening a bottle of white wine. There she is. She looks beautiful to me, but she is hard at work, the floor leader in her family restaurant. With her blond hair pulled back from her face, she comes forward to greet us with a warm smile and a hug. She is happy to receive the flowers and candy, but the dining room is slammed. Seventy five Australian seniors from a big cruise ship anchored in Split harbor are being served dinner and serenaded by a pair of traditional Dalmatian musicians dressed as sailors who wander from table to table with their guitars. Tatiana and another waiter have the entire room to manage on their own. She seats us and brings us menus, and comes by to chat, but doesn't have time to linger beyond a few pleasant words. Rudy and Anna are not to be seen. And there's no sign of Konstantin. It's clear right away that my fantasy about being welcomed at dinner for a grand reunion by the entire population of Plosnic cousins in Stobrec is not going to happen. Tatiana brings us prosciutto and seafood salad and a pitcher of white wine. We watch the elderly Australians up on their feet dancing with complete abandon to *Waltzing Mathilda*. They are dancing as if this may be the last dance in this lifetime, and they are lovely to behold.

At one of her check-ins with us at our table, Tatiana says that her husband has just returned to Dalmatia from his job in the Netherlands and has been working on a fishing boat the last few days and that the fishing, gratefully, has been good.

"Is your brother Darko here tonight?" I ask. "I would like to meet him."

"Yes, he's coming soon," she says, "with a load of fish they've caught."

Epetium is all about seafood. This is the first I've heard that Darko catches the fish in the Adriatic and brings it back to the restaurant where they grill it over wood fires. Now I know why they are closed for lunch. They are on the water fishing for dinner.

Looking around, I remember Konstantin's words about having constructed every inch of the place himself with the two hands he held in the air. For Split, a city that specializes in hole-in-the-wall restaurants, this is a large establishment, with white stone floors, a wooden bar, colorful artwork, an outdoor terrace, and a large, immaculately clean lobster tank in the middle of the room.

Tatiana is back at my side. "Try the olive oil," she's instructing me. "You did not put enough on your salad. It's very good. We make it ourselves." And she nudges the bottle of fragrant olive oil towards me. Like her father's wine, it is much fresher tasting than the olive oil I'm accustomed to at home. I pour a liberal amount over the salad, and later mop it up with the bread. The seafood salad she serves us is a sublime dish, fresh mussels and squid with risotto in a sauce of white wine and olive oil.

A man races in with a heavy cardboard box brimming with what turns out to be freshly caught red mullet. I look across the restaurant at him as he heads towards the kitchen. He is of medium height and strong build with a round face and a good head of thick brown hair. He looks like a cross between my uncle Jerry and my brother Jon. "That has to be Darko," Nat says. I am hoping he comes over to say hello but he doesn't; he's occupied.

Nat and I take photos of each other and the Dalmatian guitarists, discuss the trip just completed, the apartment we've found, and Nat's long drive back to Munich in the morning. He is going to be in Toronto in seventy-two hours and San

Francisco by the end of the week. It's been a wonderful eleven days together, an exceptional trip for a father and son.

I watch Tatiana moving around the dining room, attempting to absorb everything there is about her. She does not walk so much as scuttle, arms and legs a blur. She moves quickly and with animation. She's fast. Her quick, determined movements contrasts with my mother, who I always considered sedentary, even at times physically lazy. Tatiana is not sedentary, nor slow moving, nor lazy. She looks accustomed to managing ten jobs at once.

It is time to leave and Tatiana won't bring us a bill, despite my insistence. I tell her I am staying in Split for a few weeks and hope to see more of her family. We finally meet Darko by the door on the way out. He greets my smile with a smile of his own that seems genuine enough. When I extend my hand to shake his, he offers me his large right forearm. Same maneuver with Nat. Something about handling the fish, is our surmise. He may superficially look like my American brother and uncle, but like Konstantin, his father, Darko is a Dalmatian who has lived his entire life on the sea and has a ruddiness and physical strength that those of us who work in offices, hire help to cut our grass, and exercise only in gyms, do not possess.

"I have heard about you," he says to me.

"Yes, it was a pleasure for me to meet your father and sister," I say.

Darko mentions that he visited Chicago some years ago and stayed there with a cousin named Anton Plosnic. Did I know him?

"No, I have never heard of Anton Plosnic," I say. I don't try to explain that I don't know anyone in Chicago anymore beyond my Aunt Dorothy and a few friends from high school and have not lived there for thirty-five years.

During this exchange an obvious dynamic is on display between Tatiana and Darko. Tatiana is the baby sister and Darko the sovereign lord and undisputed head of the family with final authority in most matters. Tatiana makes an unspoken appeal to Darko to stay and talk, but he quickly excuses himself, not at all disagreeably, and strides back into the kitchen to look after his guests. Tatiana shrugs and writes down the numbers for her cell and the house phone, and the email address for the restaurant, which is the only email address she has. I promise to be in touch, and we say goodbye.

Nat and I step out into the warm night air and drive Mr. Bluey back into Split and find another parking space in the familiar confines of the Hotel Park.

"What was that all about?" I ask, confused.

"I think you've got to try to get a better idea of what is going on," he says.

When we get back to the apartment, Nat does a video question-and-answer with me standing in the kitchen in my underwear, one last piece of photographic evidence that I was once alive at 6 Tonciceva Street.

Sunshine and techno music blasting from the café downstairs awakens us the next morning. Nat assembles his gear and we walk to the beautiful waterfront promenade, the "Riva," for breakfast. Then Nat remounts Bluey and heads off for Deutschland. I am alone in Split. By the time I walk back to the apartment and check in with my laptop, I have already received a video email from Nat showing him stuck in traffic in the outskirts north of town.

So here I am, deep in the twisted maze of midlife, with exceptional health, a few kuna in my pocket, and no fixed schedule for the next three weeks. If this is not freedom I don't know what is, and if I'm not lucky then luck does not exist. My beautiful wife of thirty-five years, happy in her work and daily life, recognized the need for change in me, and graciously sent me out on this quest, but it wasn't clear if we were going to be a couple again after I returned. We were going to take it one day at a time and see where we stood with each other at the end of September. I was hoping for the best, for an honest reconciliation, that the time away would serve us well. I was thinking, certainly hoping, that our long marriage and happy family life could be restored. I did not believe, by traveling to Dalmatia, that I was saying goodbye forever to my old life while discovering a new one, but I could not be sure.

We were Tipper and Al on the local level. The kids had grown and moved out as American kids are instructed, and we were left facing each other after the long effort of having survived. Happy moments and shared activities were distant memories. Our eldest daughter was launched with an old-fashioned Virginia wedding and moved to California with her husband, our adorable youngest child was engrossed in her second year on her mountaintop at Sewanee, and Nat is returning to Germany to his work and love life. I contributed the best I could to the happiness of all. My daily duties as father were all but done. No one I could think of on the planet, not even Otis, my big black Labrador, needed me at the moment. My biological imperatives were met. My parents are both deceased. I am still loved and needed, but at this juncture, love and need require substantial revision and updating. It would be wonderful, I am certain, to love and be loved again. In other cultures, at other times in history, I'd be a barefoot holy man, my usefulness near an end. But I can feel the blood coursing through my veins. I am an eternal American optimist. I believe in continuous reinvention and personal transformation. I'll certainly get to the heart of the matter tonight with an excellent bottle of Plavac or Plavac Mali.

I find myself alone in Split because my way of dealing with being orphaned in middle age is to go away, cast myself into the unknown, and hope I'll emerge rebuilt and honest. Feeling bereft in midlife is just what happens. Dealing with it is what counts. I want to find out again who I am, if I have hard value. If I can get to the bottom of where I come from, all the better. My dear friend back home, the Star Real Estate Salesman, could not fathom my actions. He will stay in the saddle turning commissions until the Cubs win the World Series. I am the one who chose to be alone in Split. It is me who is starting over, looking for something new. Almost everyone else I know is clinging to their old lives, happy, neutral about it, or miserable. Why, I cannot say, unless it's fear that holds them there.

I want to get off the battlefield and study ancient civilizations in Dalmatia for an irresponsible amount of time. I want space and time away from home. In America, we no longer have grandparents from our village of origin showing us how to live. Grandma and grandpa are gone, shipped out to the nursing home. I don't believe Dalmatia is better than America, but it's simpler, older, and easier to comprehend. The lesson here is a course called "How to Live 101," perfect for someone like me, starting over. I vow to be an attentive student.

Deciding to get moving in the direction of the city market, I step out of my building into the palm lined square, walk twenty paces from my front door, and stand among the crowds on the busy pedestrian intersection of Tonciceva and Marmontova, the marble-paved pedestrian street. From this superb vantage point, I take in the splendid view the full length of the street down to the deep green Adriatic Sea, the big commercial ferries and small sailboats in the harbor of Split, and the hulking form of the island of Brac across the deep channel. I just stand there and take in that panorama feeling right, knowing there is nothing left behind, that it is all right here in front of me. This is the correct place. A sense of the rightness of it overcomes me. This is my season, whatever else comes later. I stand amidst these tall Dalmatians and their old stone houses bright white in the sunshine and feel intoxicated with possibility.

It's Saturday morning and Split is thick with crowds. In every third or fourth face, as has been true for me across Dalmatia, I feel a shock of recognition, the deep connection of a strong blood tie. In strangers in crowds, one after another,

I see myself, my brother, my mother, and my grandparents. I see people I want to stare at or introduce myself to or engage in conversation, as if we could naturally pick up where we left off a lifetime ago. People I know, or once knew, or could have known, are everywhere. There are couples and families and old men and women and tourists, but the congested street scene in Split this Saturday in late September consists mainly of local people. I see a pack of tall teenage boys dribbling a basketball down the street looking like future NBA stars, and many big, tough older men who looked like they once played a little basketball themselves. The women of Split are exotic beauties. Mediterranean goddesses are in every corner of the city gliding along the marble flagstones in their sandaled feet, like ocelots in their native habitat. Diocletian's Palace is a UNESCO world heritage site but it is not a museum. These ruins are inhabited.

On the way to the market I walk past a news stand with the *International Herald Tribune* staring me in the face. Out of reflex action, I catch a word or two in a headline about financial crisis and a big photograph of Bush at a news conference, but I keep moving. I am aware of events in the United States but unfazed by them, happy to be here rather than there, on the streets of Split rather than on the phone at the Big Firm telling clients over and over again, "I don't know." I am now widening my policy of highly selective media intake to include toxic people, too, if I can manage it. Toxic people will be easily avoided in Split, if only because I don't speak Croatian. I read one depressing newspaper story earlier in the week and that was sufficient. It concerned the deliberations of the Nobel Prize committee for literature. The committee found no American author qualified for the prize in 2008 because of America's "insular, isolated, vulgar" culture. America's is a "cheapening culture," the permanent secretary of the academy elaborated, as if amplification of the official statement was necessary. But sadly, I had to shake my head and agree.

The city market of Split covers a couple of acres both within and just outside the tall, thick, crumbling Roman walls. If this market were in Avignon or l'Isle sur la Sorgues it would be a starred destination, crawling with BBC film crews, Hollywood celebrities hiding behind sunglasses pinching the zucchini, and couples from New Jersey kvelling over the produce and wondering why they don't have such a market in Whippany. The market is a huge smorgasbord with separate arrondissements for fruits, vegetables, cheese, bread, baked goods and traditional cookies, meats, clothing, shoes, and antique bric-a-brac. There are also many specialty vendors of wine, olives, and olive oil. The vendors themselves, unlike, say, the vendors I've seen in the famous market at Ste-Foy-la-Grande in the Dordogne, selling expensive foie gras, truffles, and precious little packages of sea salt, are not fashionable people. They are mostly old women, real Croatian peasants, Catholic, missing a couple of front teeth, clothed head to foot in long black dresses, with a big wad of kuna tucked in their apron pocket and rolled up in a rubber band. These old ladies are not chumps. They size you up fast. When it's clear you are not from Split, they charge you an extra five kuna, and you pay and let it go, knowing you've been had by an eighty-five-year-old Croatian grandmother far more crafty than you. Croatia has not yet been admitted to the European Union, and a little harmless contraband is on sale. As you weave your way around the market these old peasant women in their black dresses hiss at you in German, "zigaretten." They have cigarettes for sale, tax-free.

The production and sale of wine and olive oil in Croatia also does not currently conform to the rules and regulations of the European Union, and this is a significant hurdle for future E.U. membership, because many Croatians, like all my relatives in Stobrec, make wine and olive oil themselves, and all producers, under the new standards, would be required to conform and become licensed. This means, in part, that the olive oil at the city market in Split is not currently offered for sale in those precious little blown-glass bottles in evidence at Whole Foods or the market in Ste-Foy-la-Grande, but instead in glass and plastic receptacles that have been used and reused many times over and that once contained whiskey, bottled water, or Coca-Cola. This is what basic, unglamorous recycling looks like, at least until Croatia conforms to all E.U. guidelines: buying fresh olive oil from a farmer from Korcula for $4 in a liter plastic bottle that says Coke Zero. This just-pressed deep green olive oil is of a luscious freshness that comes as a revelation to lovers of olive oil, but its presentation in the Split city market is none too stylish. Not surprisingly, most Dalmatians think that their wine and olive oil is without parallel and that the European Union can go stuff itself. Joining the European Union, for my family and their food and wine loving friends, means increased costs, loss of livelihood, and loss of tradition and ancient skills. And the same for NATO membership. Just having extricated themselves from the Soviet bloc, the Croats should be cut a little slack if they are none too thrilled about joining another nuclear-armed street gang right away.

It is not just the manufacture and bottling of olive oil that's at issue. The European Union, before granting membership, stipulates Croatia get a handle on its problems of organized crime and government corruption, and clean up the environment, like those massive trash heaps on the islands, which are totally incompatible with E.U. standards. We'll see how it shakes out. It will take time and will not be easy.

I buy a large wedge of delicious and unregulated cow cheese for $3 from a seventy-five-year-old woman dressed all in black; two oranges, apricots, grapes, lettuce, and one cucumber from an ancient man; a round loaf of bread from a pastry shop; some black olives, and about ten ounces of fresh olive oil in a clear glass vodka bottle for $2 from an olive oil merchant. This turns out to be enough for lunch and snacks for three days. I start heading back to the flat. I want to stop at the pharmacy. I need something to help me sleep given that I have exhausted my supply of good old American Ambien, to which I have become unwittingly addicted.

Walking in single file through the narrow passages of Split, I find myself behind yet another thug with a shaved head and hoop earring and follow him into the crowded pharmacy where there's a long, Saturday morning queue. Standing in line, I'm thinking this guy has to be Bozo's little brother, Dr. Evil's mini-me, smaller and diminished in size, pale, less threatening, without swagger, even a little wimpy, but otherwise identical. When it's his turn to speak to the pharmacist this baby thug describes his ailment and symptoms in a high-pitched whine waving his arms around his head like conducting an orchestra of complaint. He makes a purchase, turns to exit, and looks me straight in the face on the way out. It is Bozo and he's positively delighted to see me. He tells me he feels terrible, that he's come down with something awful. I'm glad to see him, too. He doesn't look like he's going to be pulling off robbery or murder anytime soon.

The pharmacist turns out to be an herbalist and she tells me they have no sleeping pills per se, no drugs or narcotics, only natural herbal products, and she shows me a bottle of a Croatian-made Valerian, which turns out to work like a charm.

After a cheese sandwich soaked in fresh olive oil in the apartment, I take a taxi into Stobrec to pay a visit to my grandmother's church. I have the driver drop me at the Stobrec campground, where I stayed in 1974, at the edge of the village, and I walk along the entire seafront, some six or seven hundred meters, taking my time, taking it all in. I have my ancestry documents in my possession in the event I meet an expert in Dalmatian genealogy.

On a hill surrounded by tall pine trees is a massive concrete bunker with gun hole ports overlooking the beachfront. I stop an older gentleman strolling along the beach and ask him about it. He tells me it's Italian, that the Italians seized control of this coast during World War II, and that it's still there because it's too expensive to take down. His English is excellent. About 100 meters further up the beach is the Bunker Restaurant.

It's Saturday afternoon but Stobrec is sound asleep. Split is alive with shoppers and gangsters and runway models and teenagers chain smoking in cafés to techno beats and motor scooters honking and weaving through heavy pedestrian traffic, but only a soul or two can be found on the streets of Stobrec. The stone church is at the top of the hill; it occupies the highest point on the rocky Stobrec peninsula. As I walk past Mornarska Street—"The Street of the Fishermen"— I stare up the hill towards the restaurant Epetium but I don't see any familiar faces. In fact, I don't see anyone at all.

My grandmother's pretty little white stone church at the crest of the hill, her place of baptism, is locked. I walk around it twice and try all of its doors and there is no one inside. A pair of older women see me trying to get in but quickly pass by without so much as a nod. I take a few photographs, stand around for a minute or two, and walk on. I find the ancient fortified wall of the original settlement built by the Greeks in 300 B.C. I walk in a circle around the entire perimeter of the peninsula, admire the jagged Adriatic coastline and translucent waters, then walk back to the Tourism Office and look around for a cab. There are none. Inside, the young Dalmatian woman behind the desk calls a cab for me. She tells me she also speaks Italian, German, French and Russian. When I tell her about trying to get into the locked church she gives me the cell phone number for the local priest. I notice, along with a few posters and postcards, that my cousin Matko Plosnic's paperback book, the *History of Stobrec*, is available for sale.

This new taxi driver looks like a professional boxer or cage fighter at the peak of his career with a bout scheduled for this very evening. His round, enormous head is shaved, polished, and deeply tanned, and he sits low in his cab in a threatening posture, like a scary hip-hop dude in D.C. No sensible person would mess with this guy on first impression alone. He is wearing gold necklaces, bracelets and rings, and a Croatian national team red-and-white checked football jersey. Black wrap around sunglasses are clasped to his scarred and pitted forehead. The hands on the steering wheel are mighty claws and his eyes are dark slits. He has a gold front tooth that glistens in the sunshine. A large black leather crucifix hangs from the rearview mirror. I would learn that a crucifix hanging from your mirror says everything about political alliances and nothing about religious faith. Almost everyone wearing a crucifix in an obvious manner, including a beautiful woman wearing one in the middle of her décolletage, is saying: I am Catholic, I am Croatian, I am a member of that tribe and those people, and I experience solidarity with you. Turns out, of course, that this guy is a perfect family man with a heart of gold who believes in God and speaks English along with several other languages. Like every other crucifix carrier I ask, he says he only goes to church on Christmas Day, if then.

I tell him I am in Split trying to plumb the depths of my ancestry, that I have an acute and overwhelming sense of déjà-vu in Dalmatia, that I can feel the Adriatic in my bones, and that I feel completely at home here. As I make this pronouncement I realize how profoundly I'm falling in love with the Mediterranean.

"I believe you," he says with a nod, his eyes widening. He tells me he just drove four generations of Croatian Americans around Split on their heritage tour.

There is a lot to this ancestor hunt. It's universal.

This tough cab driver has a word—ecomigration—that describes the plight of my grandparents and hundreds of thousands of others who left Croatia for economic reasons. It's all too familiar a concept for him. "The mass emigration from Dalmatia was a tragedy for us," he says. "We lost so many."

He offers, in a kindly enough way, that he knows everything there is to know about the United States, and thinks he has a better quality of life. "Our people are open and friendly," he says. "I love my country and my life. I have been out of the country and know what we've got here."

Of course, I would hear this refrain endlessly repeated. America is always described by these Dalmatians with exasperation, as if they really know America or could possibly be more fatigued with it than I. And it's always Kafka's Amerika, spelt with a "K." Amerika is dangerous and crazy. Germany is the most "safe" country, the most prestigious place to live in the world. And no sane, non-criminal person from any country bordering the Mediterranean ever wants to leave home. But when tough Croatian men of a certain age tell me they have been out of the country and have seen the world, I begin to get the impression that they have been out of Croatia all right, to Bosnia, Serbia, Slovenia or Montenegro, as soldiers during the last war.

If anyone in the West wants to know where all the tough white men have gone, look no further than the former Yugoslavia. The men of Croatia look like a race of giant prison guards, and at their worst, they act like goons who fail to yield even a portion of the sidewalk, mowing you down if you don't get out of their way. These guys are not appealing when first met, have no desire to win points on charm, and don't care what you think of them.

As I spend time with these men, however, I start to see myself in them, and then take strength knowing I come from such men. It's the warrior class with whom I identify, not necessarily the winemakers, farmers, and fishermen, and this surprises me at first but then it doesn't. Examining them in this way, I feel a sense of tribal connection and the intuition of past lives: that I have killed in wars of long ago with these men at my side, and that I could kill again.

Geography is your destiny. Croatia is the cruelest crossroads in all of human history. It has been conquered, occupied and stripped of its riches by the Romans, Turks, Venetians, Austro-Hungarians, Fascists and Communists. New wars may be looming. The men of Croatia, since the dawn of time, have been forced to fight on the fronts of foreign armies for the lost causes of foreign powers. These men are not softies; they will not be humiliated; they are not French. They look like men who recently won a war and are ready to fight the next. When war comes, you want these men as allies. Wars in the former Yugoslavia are not decided by unmanned drones controlled like toys by I.T. guys from distant locations. In the Balkans, soldiers wage war the old fashioned way, advancing on foot with hand held weapons and fighting from close range. These men are not going to run. They might die. But running is not an option. Every generation of these men prepare for their own war. The Croatian men will stand and fight as they always have. Observers of the recent war said that Croatian soldiers immediately sprang into action, that each solider instantly knew his military task. They look tough and self-reliant because they are. Like the British, surrender isn't in their gene pool. They live in the narrowest sliver of land between the mountains and the sea and they have no place to run. History has made them. Geography is their destiny.

Could any of these threatening guys on the streets of Split be descendants of the infamous Ustase guard from Jasenovac, the hideous Croatian concentration camp? I pray not. What do you do, it crosses my mind, if you find your people committed war crimes? What do you do if your people committed war crimes against your other people? Guess that makes you American. I later study accounts of war crimes in Yugoslavia, all the atrocities of World War II and the Wars of the 1990's, vast chronicles published online, hoping and praying not to find anyone named Plosnic, Simundza, or Blazevich listed among the accused. Their names are all clean. This is a great relief to me. Given Croatian history, it's a miracle any of my family survived. I ask them about it but they don't want to talk, not about war.

Letting myself out at the cab stand, I walk back through the sunny square crowded with Saturday shoppers into my elegant orange and yellow building. Inside, the staircase itself is a thing of beauty, with polished marble stairs, landings of old inlaid blue and white tile, ornate metal hand rails painted green, and an entire wall of frosted glass block providing ample illumination. The ground floor building directory reads like the Chicago phone book of my childhood: Vrdoljak, Buljanovic, Fazinic, Klaric.

Sitting in the sunshine on my balcony I take in the view of adjacent stone houses, the laundry drying on clothes lines, shoppers strolling in the square below, and try to convince myself that I like techno music, because techno, thumping from the big café downstairs, will be the soundtrack for my next three weeks.

A little after seven, that first dinner on my own, I wander the old town of Split in search of a place to eat. My feet are light and my heart uplifted. There is no place I have to be, no place I would rather be than this. I am neither discouraged by Darko's lukewarm greeting nor my inability to enter the church. I have only open days ahead of me to find the answers.

There is nothing else I have to do, nothing else I want to do more.

It makes sense that Darko and I cannot have a reunion if we were never together. There is no reason for him to jump out of his skin to welcome me back to Dalmatia. Why should I expect them to hail my return when they remained and had no part in my grandparent's departure? Perhaps they are about as excited to see me as my mother and Dorothy were in 1966 when they went to Stobrec and avoided everyone. My expectations of them—the love I want them to feel for me— may not be realistic. I realize it's me that needs the loving, not them.

Darko was as guarded as Konstantin was open. He looked defended, suspicious of my motives, as if asking himself: "Who is this guy and what does he want?" Perhaps that's a realistic reaction from someone put in a surreal situation.

After exploring for an hour or more, down along the Riva and through the center of the city, I find a restaurant not listed in any guidebook, a real Split hole-in-the-wall that's somehow to my liking just two blocks from my house. It's on a narrow side-street down a flight of stairs, with just four or five tables, seating a maximum of twenty, and run by a couple of guys from Split named Petar and Ivo, or, as they introduce themselves to me, Peter and John. This hole-in-the-wall is called Picaferaj, which means "The Lamplighter." It's a warm Saturday evening in September, Split is still full of tourists, it's 8:30, and I am the only guest.

When I walk in they look at me with a start, like I made a mistake, came in the wrong door, or am possibly the first customer either one of them has ever seen. When Peter, the tall waiter, asks me where I come from I first think of Richmond, the largest city near me, then opt for the next closest large city, Washington. These guys have heard of Washington. I am not sure how we get on the subject, but John, the short chef, is convinced that the events of 9/11 are entirely made-up, a complete fabrication. He's absolutely certain of it, Peter nods in agreement, and they look at me for validation. I have heard some crazy commentary about Amerika the past twelve days but I can't let this one pass. I gather up all my energy and swear to them on my life that America was attacked by terrorists on September 11th, that people I know died in New York. No, they are saying, it's a hoax. The World Trade Center is gone, I say, and the people are dead. The C.I.A. did it, John says. I am not sure how I go on with dinner after this, but I'm guessing these guys are old enough to have served in the last war and seen some atrocities in their lifetime, and that their news sources in Croatia are at least as bad as Fox Network. John opens the first of several bottles of white wine from Korcula, and the tenor of the evening improves.

The per capita consumption of wine in Croatia is among the highest in the world. Croatians drink twenty-five times the amount of wine of Americans, this according to Hugh Johnson. Croatia has seen enough of hate and drinks away its tears. They know that life is but a joke. Great, crisp, so drinkable, world class white wine from Slovenia is available everywhere for two dollars a bottle.

Of course, John and Peter ask all about my life in Washington with genuine curiosity, perhaps not seeing too many people in the Picaferaj who identify themselves as Washingtonians, and I make up answers as I go along. They ask about the size of the city, its geography, its principle body of water. Just to get back at them, I tell them that the population of Washington surpasses the entire population of all Croatia, that Washington is fifty times the size of Zagreb. They ask about the types of fish in the Atlantic and they ask what I do for a living. I don't tell them I am a ruined stockbroker. I just say that I am in "finance." This is vague enough to satisfy all of us. They want to know what I am doing by myself in Split, a tougher question to answer. I tell them that my grandmother was born nearby, and that I am getting to know family down the road in Stobrec. To which John replies: "Then you are a Croatian. You are one of us." I smile and agree. Yes, it's true, I am one of them, and proud to be so designated. Both John and Peter are smoking cigarettes like fiends throughout this entire interview.

The food at the Lamplighter proves to be better than the conversation. The handwritten menu on the black board by the front door outside listed only one dish, seafood pasta, which I request, along with a green salad. John gets busy in his kitchen, about the size of my clothes closet at home.

The seafood pasta turns out be an enormous platter of fresh mussels and shrimp purchased that morning from the city fish market in a simple olive oil sauce with spaghetti. I don't know if it's the wine or the fish or the olive oil, but I am telling them that Split has the best seafood in Europe, better than anything in Washington, and it's true. John says you can't get a slice of pizza in Paris for the price of this dinner (not true). Peter forgets to bring my salad and apologizes. He says I can still have one, but he'd have to run out for ingredients.

At the end of the evening I give John a big hug. He holds himself rigidly like a board not sure what's happening. Obviously, this American man-hug thing has not yet made it to Croatia, and John is the last Croatian man I would attempt to hug. I tell him I loved dinner and that I'll be back again soon.

I sleep late the next morning and wake to find that I have virtually barricaded myself inside the apartment with all manner of furnishings, a white plastic armchair, the metal coat rack, a large lamp, and a stack of books. In the event of a break in, I'd hear all this crashing to the floor, even mellowed out by the potent Valerian. The building is noisy at night. The big central staircase is stone and concrete and sound reverberates like an echo chamber. And of course Split is a late-night Mediterranean culture. The square outside didn't settle down until nearly 3 A.M. I don't care. I'm not here to sleep.

Stepping out onto the balcony in my underwear I can smell the essence of Split: it's the Adriatic Sea, the coffee brewing downstairs, and the city fish market just down the street. I'm not in Charlottesville anymore. Dark clouds sweep in and throw the morning's agenda into doubt, but the next moment, here comes the sun. The day is reclaimed. Life looks grand again. It's the bronze quality of the sunlight, just the right amount of warmth, and the fresh scent of the sea—that's summer in Dalmatia.

I feel far better than I deserve. I'm hungry, wide awake, and ready to get moving. The café is open but no big techno beat comes from downstairs. Must have something to do with the fact that it's Sunday. This is the final day of the antique auto show on the Riva. I intend to get some coffee, check out the old cars, and take the day as it comes.

The coolest vehicle in the show is an old Citroen H van from 1960 with a stainless steel body. I am a sucker for Citroens old and new, and this is a gem. I stick my head in the back and tell the owner, in English and sign language, that I think his vehicle is awesome. He doesn't crack a smile. He just glares at me like he wants me out of his space. Another charming Croatian guy. Must be a pal of Darko's.

The Riva is the vast sunlit stage for the ancient city of Split, its venue for concerts, the central gathering place for public celebrations, the place to see and be seen. Every restaurant is filled this Sunday morning, the entire marble waterfront promenade a happy mob scene.

I have not walked fifty paces towards the center of the Riva when Tatiana leaps out of the crowd at me from one of the big cafés. She's laughing like a kid and her smile is a mile wide. I have never, ever, been happier to see anyone.

"Dan! Where have you been? You did not call!"

She's pretending to be a scold. She is just standing there laughing. I have the feeling she was sitting, waiting, watching for me to pass by. Everyone in Split has to walk down the Riva at one time or another. She grabs me by both arms and drags me to a table littered with a dozen empty glasses where she has been sitting with a man and four women. Laughing, she forces me into a chair in the middle of this group.

I am overwhelmed by seeing her. Her sudden appearance has taken my breath away. She is my sister, my cousin, my beloved all at once, and she is my blood connection to this place. She embodies my vanished history in this ancient city of white marble. She brings the city and all that I am here to life. She also now has some claim on me. I have grown in importance to her, I can see that now. She holds my hand like she won't let me go. She's proud to show me off to her friends, and I'm pleased that my circle of acquaintance in Split will now not be limited exclusively to Bozo and his moody cousin. It's nice to meet her friends but it's better to be with her out of Stobrec, her responsibilities at Epetium, away from the dampening influence of her brother.

I can now just look at her and take her in, and touch her hand and be shocked again to see my mother in her, some Europeanized extrapolation, a relaxed Mediterranean version of my mother, who was so proud to be American, forward looking, a staunch Nixon-Agnew supporter. Now, I can admire Tatiana and see her natural smile and photograph her face from a dozen angles. It can be, for the moment, just her and I, which is what I wanted when I entered her house for the first time. Konstantin's validation of our family connection meant the world. It was the greatest gift he could give me. But Tatiana could do something else for me—she could love me in her way and let me love her back. She can accept me, as she already has. She can tell me who I once was, who I might have been. Konstantin must have seen this desire for acceptance writ large on my face.

This brilliant morning Tatiana is dressed like any southern European woman out on the boulevard enjoying a warm September day. She's wearing a stylish white shirt, blue jeans, a big leather belt, big, decorative jewelry, even a Louis Vuitton handbag, and it surprises and disappoints me a little to see her with this status symbol. She works hard in the restaurant every night, she has elderly parents and children to look after, but at the moment she is a glamorous woman from Split enjoying the sunshine, the city, and the sea.

"Tatiana, you are a woman of leisure," I tease her. "You look like a tourist."

The man in this group at the café is Vlado, Tatiana's husband, a man about her age with brown, shoulder-length hair and eye glasses with thick lenses. Vlado works in the Netherlands where he owns an antique furniture shop. He is now home for a visit of several weeks duration with Tatiana and his children. One of the women is an attractive, welcoming, elegantly attired blond named Dada, perhaps 50 years old, who also lives in Holland, is married to a Dutchman, and is, I take it, a longtime friend of Tatiana and Vlado. Sitting directly across the table from me is an alluring looking woman from Korcula with dark penetrating eyes, black hair, and olive skin, who looks like a sorcerer, a gypsy or fortune teller. This striking woman does not miss much. She's taking it all in. And then there is a young, middle-class mother from the island of Brac and her sixteen-year-old daughter. I am on my best behavior with all of them, shaking hands, bowing, catching their eye, telling them it is a great pleasure, and they are all incredibly cordial to me. But I really can't focus on any of them because of the presence of Tatiana.

I tell Tatiana that her father has enormous heart.

She looks at me with a shrug like I'm stating the obvious.

"What is life if you don't have heart?" she asks me. "Life is not worth living without heart."

This is another gift.

Every time she opens her mouth she says something that enchants me.

I can't remember the last time I heard anyone say this, if ever, and with such certainty. I hear people all the time say they can't live without a lot of cash, or that they can't live without flying first class, but the more time I spend with Tatiana, the more I love her for showing me how my family once was, before our vanities defined us, what people we are, of such strength and simplicity.

The gypsy sorcerer from Korcula has been watching our exchange closely and indicates that she wants me to lean towards her across the table, that she has something important to say to me.

"You can have her," she says to me, nodding her head with emphasis at Tatiana, "but you'll have to kill him first," nodding at Vlado, Tatiana's husband.

"That's how you do it on Korcula," I say, leaning back in my chair with a laugh, trying to make light of it.

"I do want Tatiana, and it's nice to know in your opinion I could have her, but I am not willing to commit murder. Anyway, Tatiana is my cousin."

"Yes. But a distant cousin. Separated by 100 years."

Everyone laughs. Apparently, they all know my story.

We have a pedestrian mall in Charlottesville filled with restaurants and cafés. The downtown mall is one of Charlottesville's nicest features. You may dine outside with a few friends and say hello to everyone you know who passes. The Riva in Split is the same idea, but busier, and facing the Adriatic Sea. Passersby stop and say hello and are introduced to me in turn. Several old friends of Vlado's come over to talk and shake hands, not having seen him for many months. Like in Charlottesville, everyone is talking about school and their children. The teenage girl at the table gives a bored recitation of her classes. She is friends with Tatiana's daughter Zora, and Darko's teenage son, Casimir.

Tatiana tells me about her father and brother.

She says that Konstantin is attempting to resolve property disputes concerning several parcels of vacant land he owns along the Adriatic coast in Stobrec. This is the mission he has set for himself before he dies. Tatiana's disabled mother is from Brac, and there are problems with her property there, as well. Each one of these parcels has a boundary issue with a neighbor. In order to obtain clear title to a specific plot of land, you have to get each contiguous property owner to agree to the exact lot lines. The perception of boundaries on vacant land can change over the decades, especially when neighbor's car parking areas gradually encroach onto your land. It's hard to get everyone to agree.

In addition, there is a Plosnic cousin in Chicago, now age 87, who once owned land in Stobrec on the Adriatic, which he abandoned as worthless when he left Croatia for America more than 60 years ago. Konstantin has maintained this property and paid taxes on it all the years his cousin has been gone, and is now the legal owner. Konstantin and Darko have been in contact with this elderly cousin many times, who has never expressed any interest in this property or in returning to Croatia. Darko hopes to inherit the parcel one day, but if the relative comes back during his lifetime to lay claim, he might be able to contest, or at least complicate, Konstantin's now rightful ownership.

When I appeared unannounced at Konstantin's house, Darko assumed I was a Plosnic claimant to this land, arriving to fuck things up for him.

"Wow. Thanks for telling me. That explains everything," I tell Tatiana.

Vlado has not been turned off by suggestions of his murder. He tells me about the Jugo, the warm prevailing wind from Italy (not the car), and the Bura, the cold winter wind from the hinterland. Just now on the Riva, we are experiencing a textbook example of the warm summertime Jugo, blowing up from the sands of North Africa.

Our little party starts to break up. The woman from Brac says that Brac is the most beautiful of the Dalmatian islands in the Adriatic and that I must visit. The sorcerer from Korcula tells me that Korcula is the most beautiful island and warmly welcomes all visitors. I ask her about all the abandoned houses on Korcula. She says they are abandoned no more, that they are awaiting restoration by new owners, that all questions concerning previous ownership of the properties have been resolved. She tells me I should come and buy a house on Korcula. She looks like a sorcerer but sounds like the president of the Korcula Chamber of Commerce.

"What are you going to do now?" Tatiana asks me, as we begin to head off in different directions.

"Wander around, be a tourist," I tell her.

"You should go to the beach. It's a perfect day. Go to Bacvice."

Vlado concurs.

"My father is 79," he says. "He swims at Bacvice everyday, even in winter."

"I will be here tomorrow morning," Tatiana says with a smile. "Come and look for me."

Feeling lucky, I walk back up from the Riva towards my apartment, thinking a swim at Bacvice an incomparable notion.

The famous Split fish market is still in full-swing. American fish always look in some advanced stage of decomposition whenever I see them on the ice in my local market, malodorous, headless, hacked into unappetizing filets. These fish are virtually still wriggling, their flesh vivid and rainbow-hued, their bugged-out eyes expressing degrees of shock, horror and dismay at being captured. These fish have personalities. And the only scent in this vast fish market is the fragrant scent of sea salt. The merchants display their catch on tables of pure white marble: piles and piles of bright red shrimp, angry looking scorpionfish, all sorts of bream and mullet, piles of grey mackerel that resemble anonymous salesmen from the 1950's, sole, giant tuna, and small sardines.

My long forsaken dream was to live like this on the sea. I loved Pat Conroy because my genetic make-up attached me to him and responded as only genes can to all his poetry about warm water, boats, and the Carolina lowcountry. Conroy made Charleston a true passion for me. I traveled there with my family for years and grew to love it. Conroy and I even had a passion for basketball in common. But I am thinking now that I loved Charleston and the South because they became accessible substitutes for the lost Mediterranean civilization that my genes and my bones and my soul still craved. Charleston, however, is not even a close call. There is no place in America where Mediterranean life is replicated.

The email I composed read as follows:

Dear Darko

It was a pleasure for my son and I to meet you at
Epetium. We had a wonderful dinner. Thank you for
your hospitality.

Please understand that I want nothing from you.
My family in the USA lost contact with everyone
in Croatia a very long time ago. My only wish is to
know where we come from, for myself and for my
three children.

I hope to spend some time next week in the Split
archives and the church in Stobrec researching family
history. So you may see me in Stobrec next week.
Your father is a jewel. Please thank him for his
kindness.

I hit "send."

Then I put on a tee-shirt, swimming trunks, and sneakers,
and head off through the crowds again in the direction of
Bacvice Beach, a ten minute walk. I am strolling in the sunshine
through the center of a major European city in swim trunks
and sunglasses, with a towel draped over my arm, and in ten
minutes I will be waist-deep in the Adriatic Sea surrounded by
old men and naked young women.

In an isolated park between the bus station and the beach
I see a pair of unkempt men sitting at a wooden picnic table

taking turns swigging from a brown paper bag. These are the first real derelicts I have seen in all Dalmatia. The population of the hopeless and disenfranchised in Charlottesville is far greater than it is here. Charlottesville, not long ago, was named the best place to live in America by a poll or magazine, but we have more panhandlers, homeless people, volatile public drunks, aggressive beggars, disabled veterans in wheelchairs, and people picking through trash bins than I can ever remember.

At Bacvice, I look across the deep, healing Adriatic waters—"the immense volume of the sea's breathing," as Lawrence Durrell called it—and lay my towel on a beach that is equal parts sand, gravel, and crushed cigarette butts. Later, I move over to the concrete walkway with deeper water favored by more solitary types and the senior citizens of Split. I can sun and read here, and dive from the walkway into the sea. I feel the play of the Adriatic, rising and falling upon my back and neck. An hour in the Adriatic every day, an olive oil-based diet, as little worry as possible, plenty of good wine, taking life one day at a time, and I'll be a new man. My waistline, I think, is shrinking before my eyes. If only I could get these Croatians to stop smoking indoors, stop using the beach as an ashtray, and to properly dispose of trash and litter, then we'd have a proper E.U. candidate.

The Adriatic is a small sea—an Airbus can fly across it from Split to Ancona, Italy, in eighteen minutes—but for my family it is an entire world.

The satellite television in my yellow apartment picks up a hundred channels or more. I avoid CNN, I don't want to know what is going on in America, and especially avoid CNBC, because I don't want to absorb all the inaccurately reported bad news from Wall Street. Plus, I'm fatigued with the sweat-soaked CNBC talking heads, shrieking at one another. Besides, I live in a three room apartment on the Adriatic. What do I care about stocks? And there is nothing I can do about any of it. I opt instead for the dulcet tones of the BBC as I settle down to a dinner of salad, bread, and cheese, all bathed in olive oil, and bottles of water and white wine.

The broadcast tonight concerns the telegenic British celebrity cookbook author Nigella Lawson, the so-called "queen of food porn," and her search for her Jewish ancestors in Spain and the Netherlands. Nigella is not only smart and beautiful, she was born rich, heir to the J. Lyons Company, once one of the largest restaurant chains in Britain. Now she's passionate about getting to the bottom of her family history. Nigella is slightly younger than I, just the right age to take a serious interest in a mature subject. I sit up in my chair.

Nigella tirelessly crisscrosses Europe for months in search of an answer. She wants more than anything to be descended from Sephardic Jews from Spain, about whom she has spun a romantic fantasy. It turns out that her chief ancestor was Ashkenazi, not Sephardic, an apprentice shoe maker who fled The Hague for England after being convicted of a minor theft and sentenced to an eighteen-month jail term. This was not the conclusion Nigella sought, but she was happy with what she found. Generations later, her family thrived. That trip her great, great grandfather made fleeing jail time in The Hague was the most important step anyone had ever taken in the history of her family.

After 10 P.M., virtually all the satellite channels turn into porn, as if on autopilot, and they make for diverting viewing for at least five minutes before I fall asleep.

———◦◦◦———

The next morning, from my terrace vantage point above the cafés in the square, begins cloudy with gusty winds, with autumn knocking loudly for admission, knowing it cannot be held at bay forever, that its time is coming. Like great armies, summer and fall are going to fight it out over Split in the next few weeks, with one gaining ground then the other dominating for a few days more. The water temperature in the mighty Adriatic starts to show the effects of this battle, proving that a deep body of water, with tides and strong currents, is far from immune from the sudden onslaught of dark clouds and gusting winds. Split is paradisiacal in summer. But winter, even with warm respites from time to time, can feel downright northern European. The Bura and the relentless cold rain turns this outside city indoors. Split will go 100 days without rain in the summer and fall, and 100 consecutive days of steady rain December through February. But this morning, at least, after inconclusive skirmishes and dramatic skies, here comes the sun. It's going to be another exquisite day after all. Fall will just have to wait his turn, and no one is sorry to see him go.

The historic archives of the city of Split, or what little is left of them after the Communists destroyed most records in 1948, are held in a large modern depository called the Optina Grad Split, a combination municipal office building and warehouse, located in an eclectic and somewhat shabby residential neighborhood in the eastern hills of the city, about a twenty minute walk all uphill from my apartment. Even after the exertions of the recently completed bike trip, I am being overtaken on the broken stone sidewalk by a succession of old women, gripping shopping bags full of purchases from the city market, who climb these hillside staircases with far greater alacrity than I. While I stop to catch my breath, the old grandmothers keep moving past. Don't these old ladies know they are supposed to be in a nursing home somewhere sitting in a wheelchair watching television?

In the long dim entry chamber of the Optina Grad Split, two fatigued male apparatchiks sit behind tiny Tito-era desks each piled three feet high with frayed documents. It's just past 9 A.M. and they already look hostile, like a pair of beaten junkyard dogs. Not everyone in Dalmatia is healthy and robust looking. There is not a computer to be seen anywhere in this vast hall. It appears this beleaguered duo is processing these stacks of faded documents by hand. One of the officials impatiently peers up at me from his desk, seems to comprehend the nature of my inquiry, and vaguely directs me to the third floor, to turn to the right, and go to the end of the corridor. As instructed, I climb the staircase, gaze down the long eerie corridors, open the correct door, switch on the overhead lights, and choke on the dust inhaled into my lungs. The key to my family history might indeed be somewhere in this vast gray storage room, in one of thousands of filthy cardboard boxes, but with no Croatian language skills I was not going to find it on my own, and the dull apparatchiks downstairs were not there to help me. Shuffling through these papers would make you sick. The place stunk of death. So I left.

I am back among the food stalls of the city market with its pungent local wines, late harvest, and the last of the summer fruit and vegetables. Garlic merchants from the mountains have appeared displaying their produce in long gray ropes of bulbs braided together by their long stems. I purchase oranges, apricots and grapes from an elderly woman all in black who sized me up fast and added an extra five kuna to the amount owed. Then I head down to the Riva in search of Tatiana.

It's all about Tatiana.

In the end, Tatiana is enough.

The discovery of Tatiana is like finding I am related to Melina Melcouri in *Never on Sunday* or the young Sophia Loren as she appeared in *Two Women*, someone emblematic, deeply rooted to a place. To possess such a beauty as a blood relative in a distant land is like receiving a rare, unexpected inheritance, a bequest of enormous magnitude. In Tatiana's face I see the mysteries and secrets of my ancient ancestry and origin on display. She holds the answers I seek in her limbs and breasts and hair. She is the truth of who I am. She and I have sprung from the same waters. Looking at her, I feel valuable and connected to a people and a place, finally like I belong.

Tatiana, stunningly, also gives me the gift of another chance with my mother. Through her I have a window into my mother, and can see my mother as a woman, young and vital. I can look at Tatiana with frankness and admire her in a way I could never have permitted myself with my mother. Knowing Tatiana, just being with her, will help me forgive, accept, and love my mother again.

This entire package is so incandescent and electrifying that I want to explain to her what's happening to me but cannot; I want to apologize for it but don't have the ability or the words. I want to tell her that in America we make a virtue of eradicating the past, as if our bright future depends upon it, with the result that no one knows who they are anymore, that everyone's adrift. No one has a clue where they come from, beyond a few broad strokes, and no one cares, because they bought into the big fantasy that progress is more important than authenticity. Or they make up whatever stories suit them about their past, or sound good in the retelling.

But the fact is, I am not so ignominious after all. I am not the assimilate rejected by the doctrinaire Highland Park rabbi. I am not the Big Jew as portrayed by my pals in Charlottesville. Without such self-knowledge, I had allowed myself to be painted in a corner and construed in such a way. I had even allowed myself to be employed for years by an institution I ceased to believe in because I never knew who I was and where I came from. For all this I blame no one but myself.

Tatiana sees me on the waterfront before I see her. She's walking towards me with an easy smile and wraps a bare arm across my shoulders and brings me to her table. Her elegant friend Dada is drinking white wine with two more Dalmatian women, another mother-teenage daughter combination. Tatiana, I'm finding, is intensely social, like my youngest daughter. She is never alone, always surrounded by a pack of friends.

I tell her about my failed visit to the city archives and my unsuccessful attempt to gain entry to the church in Stobrec. With trepidation, I ask about the family friend I met and if he had success looking into my background. She says they have heard nothing from him, that she does not know if he even made an effort. Of course, my family history matters mostly to me. It's up to me alone to find out the truth. I started this journey as a trip of renewal and rejuvenation in the country of my grandparent's birth, but now I have work to do.

We sit talking for two hours, drinking wine and sparkling water in the pure white sunshine, sharing a bowl of mussels, listening to the clinking of ice in glasses around us. We are the only people on the Riva not smoking cigarettes. She and the glamorous Dada talk endlessly about food, about fish, about making wine and olive oil. Tatiana says that taking all meals is not compulsory and not good for you. I tell her little Rudy needs a computer. She does not agree. She does not want her son sitting glazed and sedentary before a screen, disconnected from people, lost in cyberspace. She tells me that her attitude is not as severe as Konstantin, who distrusts all technology, even though she and all the rest of them are clearly addicted to their cell phones. Our conversation all in English pushes her language skills to the maximum and she starts to flag. Tatiana is not language-centric in any case, not one who devotes all her energy to the spoken word. When a song she likes starts playing from the café, she dances and shakes it up in her chair, singing along. She loves music. It's OK with her just to be.

Not for the first time I think, I don't miss Charlottesville. I don't want to go home.

Tatiana says they are planning something for me in the next few days. They want to take me somewhere special. Then she excuses herself; she's got an elderly aunt in Stobrec that needs attention and she must go.

When I get back to the apartment I find the following email message waiting for me:

Dear Dan,
I am looking forward to seeing you again.
I am in the restaurant every evening, so you can
come and we can meet.
Tatiana will help you as much as she can.
So, see you in Stobrec and kind regards.
Darko

This is a good moment. I feel it all turning in my direction.

I walk back to Bacvice through the busy pedestrian zone in my bathing trunks holding a towel. No one looks at me twice. The beach is active, the sea cooler by one degree. I jump in feet first from the concrete walkway, then swim side and breast stroke all the way out to the restraining rope which protects swimmers from the strong currents of the open channel. Then I return and lay on my back on the concrete walkway. An old man sunning himself on a nearby bench releases an astonishing fart, loud and long, a fart from a Chaucerian tale, another reminder that I am not in France.

Dinner in the apartment *tout seul*, the French windows open wide to my terrace balcony with the curtains billowing in the breeze, and the comforting crowd noise and the tinkle of glassware from below. I think: city life is so agreeable. I have more cheese and bread and fresh fruit for dessert and sparkling water with lemon and the amusements of my own company.

The television programming again was created as if with me in mind. The BBC this evening is featuring another hour long installment of its program entitled "Who Do You Think You Are?" The hero tonight is Jeremy Irons, attempting to discover his roots in Ireland, who declaims, sounding a little like Claus von Bulow, a little like Scar from the *Lion King*: "Whenever I go to West Cork I feel at home. Why?"

Why? Because it turns out Irons is indeed from West Cork, on his father's side, six generations deep into the past. His intuition about his connection with this locale was uncanny. In his certainty I saw my own powerful response to the Adriatic shore at Stobrec. Unlike Nigella Lawson, he found precisely what he wanted and was thrilled with his discovery.

Before the cameras, Irons takes a genealogical journey to Yorkshire, Dublin, Northern Ireland, and back to West Cork.

He interviews the polite custodians of parish records and the charming vicars of Irish churches who bend over backwards to help this handsome superstar puzzle out his ancestry, not exactly my experience this morning with the surly apparatchiks in the Optina Grad Split. I was faced with a dark and cavernous warehouse full of filthy boxes. The officiants and church figures helping Irons were deeply honored to be so engaged. They got to shoot a film sequence for the BBC with Jeremy Irons. The scary part of the whole episode is that Irons was already living in West Cork for years, just twenty miles from the original home of his great, great, great, great grandfather.

Many, it seems, are involved in this process, Nigella Lawson, Jeremy Irons, the BBC, and all the subscribers to ancestry. com. Months later, at Nat's urging, I submit a spit sample to 23andme, *Time* magazine's "Invention of the Year." Fill a test tube with saliva, mail it to the company's lab in Mountain View, and your genetic profile and DNA ancestry are returned in the form of a highly detailed 20-page report. Despite the $400 charge, there is a ten-week wait for results.

The young pastor in my grandmother's church is a newcomer to the village. He is not Dalmatian, and he is not popular with the old families of the ancient peninsula. Tatiana and Vlado have nothing good to say about him, just as they refuse to acknowledge other newcomers from the hinterland. Me, on the other hand, I am now one of them, so they share with me their confidences and stories of their lives. The village church of Stobrec is just one hundred meters from Tatiana's house. My grandmother lived in a stone house on the seafront, according to my Aunt Dorothy, and walked to this church every Sunday. She was baptized there on Christmas Day, 1888. I dreamt about the distance from her house to the church, and how many times she made this walk.

After coffee downstairs in the café the next morning, I call the priest from my computer. The poor man does not speak English and is receiving his first phone call on Skype, a lethal combination. Fortunately, he has an English-speaking assistant in the room and he passes the phone to her. After a full minute of complete confusion, she tells me that the priest is in church every afternoon and I am welcome to visit anytime.

Then, even though I know it is now the middle of the night, I call Dorothy in her nursing home on the north side of Chicago hoping that she has not died since I spoke with her last.

"Hello?"   It's her gruff voice, sounding sleepy and disoriented.

"Dorothy, I apologize for waking you. This is your nephew Dan. I am in Split and I am calling you from my computer on something called Skype which has a bad delay and which makes my voice sound garbled."

"You sound terrible. Are you sick? Are you in trouble?"

"No, I'm fine. This is just the way my voice sounds on Skype."

"Telephones are so terrible these days. Whatever happened to good telephones?"

"Dorothy, I want you to know that I have met several of our relatives and cousins in Stobrec and I have been spending time with them."

"Well, you better keep your wallet zipped. You are just a rich American sucker to them. They'll tell you some sob story and ask you for money. And I'm sure we don't have any relatives there anymore. All of our relatives are dead. None of them could have survived the Nazis and the Communists."

"Dorothy, there may be seventy or eighty of them, and they appear to be thriving."

"What?"

And I tell her the entire story. It's 3 A.M. Chicago time.

We speak for an hour, the longest conversation Dorothy and I have ever had. At the end of the call she says: "I wish I could go there."

"Dorothy," I tell her. "These are beautiful people. We can be proud of who we come from."

"Wonderful," she says. "So wonderful."

Five

THE MOUNTAIN PARTY

Tatiana is accompanied by an even larger entourage on the Riva this morning. I'm late. Tatiana beams up at me and pats the empty chair next to her. She is with the easy-going Vlado, who understands that Tatiana is the linchpin to my happiness; blond Dada, who loves to party at any hour; Sasha, Dada's pale, blond, long-haired son who has a wild look in his eyes; and Layla, Sasha's pretty wife from Bosnia, Sarajevo to be precise, a city with a most terrible history, none worse anywhere in the world. Dada, I learn, is one hundred percent Bosnian herself, from the city of Tuzla, another of the sorriest places on the planet. No wonder Dada likes to party. She witnessed firsthand the Tuzla massacre of 1995, she tells me later in a whisper.

Also joining us is a large man with a big head of wavy brown hair and mustache sitting at the end of the table wearing one of those ubiquitous red-and-white-check Croatian national soccer team jerseys, as symbolic in sports-mad Split as a crucifix. This tough, athletic-looking man, Vlado tells me, is a Plosnic on his mother's side, a former professional soccer player, and a "big wheel in Stobrec employing a lot of people." "Big wheel" and "Stobrec" would seem to nullify each other, but I keep my opinion to myself. Vlado is the best English speaker of the group. He is generous and attentive to me, translating conversations with care, answering all my nonstop, deeply personal questions while the others are caught up in the fun.

This congregation is in high spirits when I arrive. Dada has been staying with Tatiana in one of the guest rooms above the restaurant in Stobrec, and her son Sasha and daughter-in-law Layla are staying up in the mountains in the remote country retreat of a musician named Dundo, whom I would meet later that week. It is a sunny, breezy morning on the waterfront promenade, the temperature a degree or two cooler than the day before. Everyone is wearing a sweater now, or a windbreaker or fleece.

The new people around the table look at me with curiosity and want me to recite the story about how I found Tatiana and her father. I tell them that it was fate that brought me to Tatiana, and now that I have found her I am never going to let her go, and they laugh wildly at this version of our improbable connection. But I don't want to chat with them at the moment, however kind they are to me. I want to bask in the sunshine with Tatiana. I want her to tell me everything about her life, about who she is, no detail is too small. I want to forge a link with her. I want to hear everything she has to tell me about our family history while we have this chance. It's not hard to get her going.

She starts in on her marriage to Vlado.

Vlado is from Split; both parents are still living. She and Vlado met in the Split central high school and married when she was 21, he 23. Vlado is a great and good husband and father but his issue is work. He's too emotive, he needs a change but won't make it, his business is not doing well, the escalating costs, the distance from home, raising the children on her own while taking care of her mother, the narrative spills from her. She wants Vlado to return home from the Netherlands and return to hair styling, his previous occupation. Their seventeen year old daughter Zora is going to begin school for hair styling soon, and she and her father can open their own shop in Stobrec, that Vlado can teach Zora the business, but Vlado has no such desire.

Then she turns to Konstantin. She is completely exasperated by her father. He constantly complains, he talks ceaselessly about politics, crime and corruption. She wishes he would just be quiet and play his music. That's the role of music. Why does he not understand that? Living under the same roof with three generations of family has its complications, it appears.

The thought crosses my mind that Dorothy might be right about their negative carping. But I think: this is how they communicate, they grumble, they like to complain. So do most human beings.

The very next minute Tatiana is dancing like a kid in her chair singing along with a tune being played outdoors at the café, the litany of problems gone, vanished into thin air.

Dada's blond son Sasha and his dark wife Layla get up from the table and say good bye to us. They are catching one of the big commercial ferries from the port of Split to the island of Hvar where they are spending the night and they are excited to be going. They also live in the Netherlands and are touring around Dalmatia this week.

As soon as they leave I tell Dada that her son and daughter-in-law make an attractive couple. I tell her that my eldest daughter was just married to a young man who I care for, that it was important for me to love my son-in-law.

"Sasha almost married an Iranian and spent three months with her living in Tehran," Dada said. "I celebrated when they broke up. Layla's first boyfriend was an Albanian who did not finish school."

Vlado tells me with a grin that they have planned a party for me tomorrow night at a special place, and to meet them at the restaurant in the evening.

"A beautiful place," Tatiana says with emphasis. "You will like it."

"What can I bring?" I ask.

"A smile," Dada tells me.

As we stand and get ready to part company, the man in the football jersey, the Big Fixer of Stobrec, a man of about my height and weight, ambles over and stands facing me only inches from my nose. I have been aware of his quiet scrutiny of me for this hour on the Riva.

"You look like a Plosnic," he says gravely. "You are obviously Dalmatian. You are more Dalmatian than American. You are one of us."

Then this big, tough-looking former pro soccer player grips me in his arms and kisses me on both cheeks.

"Any man in search of his origin and ancestry is on a holy quest," he tells me. "I am glad you found us, because we are all one family. You are part of us and we are part of you."

"Thank you so very much," I tell him, still in his clutches, averting my head but our noses touching. "I am deeply honored."

"A man must have a base or he is nothing," the Big Fixer says with casual assurance, as if he has made this obvious point a million times before.

Tatiana, Vlado and the Big Fixer all smile and wave goodbye. Until tomorrow night. It looks like I've got myself a new family, a whole new tribe.

———

Dorothy reminded me to visit the Mestrovic museum in Split, and I decide to walk there now, about two miles from the Riva. Ivan Mestrovic is arguably the most famous artist in the history of Croatia, one of the greatest sculptors of religious subjects since the Renaissance. I remember, from my boyhood in Chicago, his massive bronze statutes, The Bowman and The Spearman, in Grant Park, which made such an impression on me. This walk from the center of Split to the Mestrovic museum is also one of the most scenic walks in the city, through the wooded, seaside park called the Marjan, the most exclusive neighborhood in Split, with large villas with Porsches and

Ferraris parked in front. If I narrow my focus, I could be on the French Riviera, in Cap Ferrat. The Marjan has been in use as a park since the third century A.D., laid out by Diocletian himself, who created it as recreation space for the 10,000 inhabitants of his walled city. Tito loved the Marjan too, and built his summer home here, the Vila Dalmacija, which is still standing on a glorious site overlooking the sea. The spectacular house of contemporary design with tennis court next door to the Mestrovic mansion is the residence of Split native Goran Ivanisevic, the Wimbledon champion of 2001, who now spends most of the year in Monte Carlo. At least Ivanisevic has a home here. Basketball great Toni Kukoc, some Dalmatian men complain to me, spends too much time on the North Shore of Chicago. In any case, the museum is breathtaking and the walk through the Marjan, with its pine forest, magnificent views, and crescent beaches, one of the highlights of my stay. If I am going to buy a retreat for myself in Split, I conclude, the neighborhood around the Marjan is the first place to look.

On my walk back into the city center, in my euphoria after the events of the morning, I lose my resolve and buy a copy of the *International Herald Tribune*, with alarming news covering the front page. I am sorry I bought it seconds after scanning the headlines. Its entire coverage is about financial panic in the U.S.A. The Dow industrials have now fallen 1,700 points since the demise of Lehman. One article is entitled "Present at the Crash," where the writer portrays himself as a wizened financial hero, even at the age of 23, his first ritual baptism by fire, and it's all so terrible but so cool.

Reading this, I am acutely aware—having left the Big Firm three weeks ago—that if I were to tell the Branch Manager today I was leaving, after such a rapid worsening of conditions, he would say: so long, adieu, and happily show me the door with no pomp and ceremony. There would be no gala farewell at the C&O, no speeches and gifts, no clients dressed up and happy for me to be leaving, no support staff nibbling the finger food—it would be: don't let the door hit you on the way out. But I am apprehensive because I don't understand the situation, no one quoted anywhere in the paper makes any sense, and no one knows what it will take to stop, or how low will it go. The rumor of the day is that Washington Mutual, a great American financial institution for decades, is on the verge of declaring bankruptcy. Washington Mutual going belly up is unthinkable. Terrible rumors are in circulation. I was feeling a lot better before looking at the newspaper. But that's part of being American: find a news item that makes you feel miserable, and when that source of misery runs its course, find something else to be miserable about.

The sports and arts sections and the news from the Obama campaign all make diverting reading, but I avoid glancing at the stock tables. I don't need to know what has happened to share prices, it can only negatively effect my attitude and time away, and there is nothing I can do about any of it.

It's clear we Americans are taking this hard. We don't do well if you take away our money. Most of us have no fallback position, few tangible skills beyond shopping and credit card swiping. The privileged wives of a few clients would call in

distress when the swipe bar from their Big Firm credit card had
worn off. Could I get them a new card? ASAP?

It's all about quick access to your money. Fair enough. But
what if there was no cash left to access? Big trouble.

The distance between making that kind of call to your
broker and learning to become resilient enough to take charge
of your life during a downturn is unimaginably vast. However
nauseated this collapse makes me, I take strength witnessing a
simpler life in Dalmatia, knowing I come from four immigrant
grandparents who came to the U.S.A. on a bold gamble with
nothing but the clothes on their backs, and that my parents,
born to them on the south side of Chicago, began their lives in
the 1920s, 1930s, and 1940s, in rented rooms with no money.
At this particular moment in history I might be rich in relative
terms, but in terms of the long history of my family—from the
Jews of my father in The Pale of Settlement to my fishermen
ancestors on the stony Adriatic—we have been poor much
longer than we have been rich.

In Dalmatia, among the connections on my mother's side,
I am getting a lesson about how to live well, not just with
less, but well, period. This lesson, it appears, is coming at an
opportune moment. And it's built on the foundation of family
and community.

About halfway back to the apartment, I stop at a sidewalk
café on a quiet side street in the shade and sit down next to four
elderly men drinking plum brandy and playing a card game,
with two or three onlookers, including the neighborhood
police man on foot patrol, standing over their shoulders,

watching the action. I order a cup of coffee and read the grim newspaper. Almost immediately, a fight breaks out among the card players with two men nearly coming to blows. A man with snowy white hair, a guy older than Konstantin, is outraged. He has been cheated by the bald man with eyeglasses seated across from him and suddenly starts to bellow. He is threatening and screaming at his adversary, veins enlarged in his neck, slamming his fist down on the wooden table. They don't appear to be gambling for money; I don't get what the fuss is about. The policeman watches the action with a smile and walks inside the café. This coarse scene, like the old man cutting world-record farts at the beach, was so non-French and non-Parisian as to be noteworthy. Back in the yellow apartment, I take a nap before returning to the church in Stobrec.

Branko Stepinac is a Catholic priest with a grave demeanor and the assignment of a small church in an ancient village to which he has no personal connection. He is not a big Croatian manly man and he is not a Mediterranean-Italian looking Dalmatian. He is from Zagreb, has dense black hair and black eyebrows, a round, studious face, a pale complexion, and the lean look of a man with something to prove, who knows he has an uphill fight on his hands. Simultaneously, he has the air of detachment and resignation typical of priests in service to God continuously disappointed by the failures and foibles of men. This occupational hazard is compounded in his case by a lack of credibility among the established families and uncertainty how to rebuild the once thriving congregation. Of course, many churches in the former Yugoslavia, despite all the crucifixes on display, do not have thriving congregations. In me, he sees the chance to prove himself at once with all ten Plosnic households of Stobrec, and he would like nothing more than to be of help. When I walk in and introduce myself, he comes to life. His assistant is a sweet young woman from the village, a volunteer, and a first year student at the university in Split. Her English is limited, but she is patient and unembarrassed and laughs with charm at her mistakes. The three of us sit in a shaft of light in the nave of my grandmother's church, which could not accommodate more than sixty or seventy worshippers. The priest is attired his in High Catholic best: an immaculate floor-length black robe with white collar and an ornate silver crucifix hanging from a thick silver chain around his neck.

Dripping with formality, he introduces himself to me as Don Branko, and indicates that he has already seen Paulina's birth certificate. Konstantin brought it to him last week, along with the copies of my other documents.

He gazes at me and says, after a moment of reflection: "You may be American but you look like a young Konstantin. The resemblance is amazing."

I am grateful for this compliment. I am young relative to Konstantin, perhaps, but increasingly the senior one wherever I go. I am somewhere on the back nine, that much is for certain, maybe the 12th or 13th hole, if I'm fortunate. I was the oldest guy on the bike trip, but at least I was on the bike trip.

"I have been to the house and seen the family photographs," Don Branko continues. "You do indeed look like Konstantin when he was young. You have the same skin and the same eyes, but most especially it is the shape of your face. It is long and thin like Konstantin's face. The construction of your body is also like his. It's very clear that you are Dalmatian and a Plosnic of Stobrec."

This is about as much validation as anyone could have hoped for, the second time today I have been described in such a manner by someone who previously had never met me.

"Tatiana is my mother reborn," I tell him. "The way she walks and speaks, the way she looks, everything about her is my mother," I tell him.

Except that Tatiana, with less time, privacy and space than my mother, fewer clothes, even without a new Mercedes every two years, and a sick parent with a terrible illness, a husband with no job security, even with all this she is still somehow happier than my mother was, and I think of this with sadness. Tatiana is Dalmatia undiluted, which does not mean that Tatiana is perfect. But it does mean that Tatiana isn't trying to look like Jennifer Aniston, or, in the case of my mother, Marilyn Monroe. It means that Tatiana can be herself, rather than feel compelled to style herself after a Hollywood prototype, which my mother and her peers bought into, and which only further distanced them from the truth of who they are.

"Then you must tell Tatiana that you love her," the Priest is telling me, "and by doing so, love your mother again."

This probing insight I did not expect from this placid-looking priest. I slump back into the oak pew. His round face is serene, his expression as tranquil as the Adriatic at low tide. I look at the 19-year-old translator and wonder if she understands a word she has uttered, not to mention the poetry of it. And I consider the rightness of what he has said. I never made peace with my mother, and I never felt her love of me. I could tell Tatiana I love her, but I need Tatiana to tell me she loves me, as I needed my mother to love me, and that's too much to ask of her or anyone.

My mother was a classic Dalmatian beauty. She worked as a model in the early years of her marriage and had the narcissism that often accompanies great beauty. But physical affection—for mom—was unseemly; it would mess with her makeup. Watching Tatiana fuss and fawn over her son Rudy, touching, holding him to her, stroking his hair, kissing him noisily on his cheeks, made me think: this is how a boy-child should be adored by his mother. Here on the Adriatic, they haven't forgotten the basics of loving one another.

So what am I supposed to do now? Explain the deficiencies of my American upbringing to Tatiana? And hope that she understands it, rather than thinking me crazy? Did I really think that Tatiana could put this right for me?

But Priest Don Branko's hunch was correct. Any man my vintage traveling back in time to a village church looking for answers was running on empty.

My mother's given name was Goldie, a name of hope conferred upon her by immigrant parents so recently settled in the big Croatian neighborhood near St. Jerome's. Goldie was a daring American name for a little girl born into a new world. There are traditional names for girls in Croatia like

Mara, Theresa, and Ivana, but Goldie was as American as you could get.

Of course Goldie was too unsophisticated a name for my rapidly Americanizing mother, who rechristened herself Veronica, then Ronnie, as she grew up in Chicago. We celebrated mom's birthday on the fourth of July. Only years later did I find her birth certificate recorded her actual birth date as July 3. The subtle remaking of her past in the U.S.A. had begun. In innocent details she showed me it was permissible to manipulate the facts to suit one's sense of self. In 1950s America, Ronnie was about as cool as it got. If you changed your name and your birth date, did that mean you were a fraud? Or did it just go with the territory of being a new American, in a place where no one knew your history?

I am sure I am being too hard on my mother. Even James Salter changed his name. If Norma Jeane Mortenson could become Marilyn Monroe, then Goldie could become Ronnie. And name changing was nothing compared with the rampant cosmetic procedures of the next generation. But it's an American activity, and I may be sensitive to it because so many Jews (like Salter) assumed Waspy names and identities. Just because you call yourself Nathanael West doesn't mean you cease to be Nathan Weinstein. You can only distance yourself so much from the truth of who you are before you become disconnected and inauthentic.

"Family history is the individual's inescapable destiny," Father Branko is saying through the filter of his teenage translator. "We can separate ourselves by centuries and thousands of miles but we are still exactly the same. Life gives us many second chances, and it is never too late to find peace."

Priest Don Branko leads us into his office at the rear of the church, a small room of white stone, no more than twelve feet square, with an old oak desk with a clean tabletop and empty oak book cases lining the walls from floor to ceiling.

"These book cases," Don Branko is saying with a wave of his hand, "were once filled with ledgers with all the recorded history of the entire village going back to the beginning of recorded time, all its birth documents, baptism records, marriage certificates, and notations of death. All we have left now is this one thin volume. The rest of them were confiscated and destroyed by the Communists in 1948, and not just in our church, but in all the churches of Yugoslavia."

"But you, somehow, you are in luck," he says to me, removing the solitary leather bound volume from the shelf, "because there is something in this for you." And after a few seconds of muttering to himself and turning the heavy smudged pages, he shows me the entry for Paulina's birth, October 21, 1888.

"Her father and mother were Ivan and Ivanic Plosnic, as you know, and, as you can see, here," pointing to another line item entry in black ink, "Paulina's father Ivan was also himself born in Stobrec in 1856, and that his own father, Paulina's grandfather, named Mate, was also born here in the village in 1830. Mate's father, Paulina's great grandfather, and your great, great, great grandfather, he was named Ante, and he too was born in this village, although his birth year is missing. These are the only records we have for your family. We are very fortunate to have them. How this last volume escaped destruction is unexplainable, for a church this age must have had hundreds of such volumes, and all of them are gone but this one."

These church records links me to the village of Stobrec circa 1800. Somehow I am composed enough to ask about the events of 1948.

"The Communists destroyed everything and made attendance in church illegal."

"But family records, why would those be destroyed?"

"The crimes committed by the Communists in many countries had no logical explanation. They were afraid even of the deceased."

This last statement is beyond my comprehension.

"It is my understanding," he continues, "that the Plosnic family is among the earliest families in Stobrec. We know that there was very limited mobility in the early 19th century. The mass emigration from Dalmatia did not begin until the mid-1890's. With your great, great, great, grandfather born here around 1800, it is very likely, or at least quite reasonable to speculate, that your family was here for much longer, perhaps as far back as the 17th century, or even earlier. I am absolutely certain, but can not prove, that you are related to Tatiana and Konstantin, because all the families named Plosnic in Stobrec blossomed from the same seed. That much is common knowledge."

In response, I tell Don Branko that I found the warehouse in the Optina Grad Split, and that it was a formidable obstacle for me with no ability in the Croatian language.

"You would have found nothing of value in that warehouse. All records in the Split archives are gone. All the records for the municipality of Split were destroyed after the Communists came to power. All the city records of taxes paid, houses bought and sold, crimes, jail sentences, school prizes—even all of this was destroyed."

"Then how does someone like me interested in authenticating their background get to the bottom of it?"

"By doing what you are doing. By personal connection with relatives who know the whole story about their families."

Taking a deep breath, I know it is time to leave.

Tatiana and her father accepted me immediately and without a moment's hesitation. Tatiana told me the morning I met her, standing in her front hall, and the priest confirmed today, that all Plosnics in town are related to one another, from the beginning of recorded time. The Big Fixer of Stobrec, no romantic pansy, no fabulist, kissed me on the Riva without benefit of alcohol. What more do I want? That's enough. Let it go. I have my answer, and the answer is good. This is my ancestral home, this village of white stone on the blue-green Adriatic Sea, these are my people, this is where I come from.

Getting up, I thank the priest and his young assistant for all their time and effort. I am deeply touched.

"I am but a newcomer to this old village," Don Branko Stepinac says to me in his somber tone at the church door in parting, "but I have learned a traditional expression we have here which applies to you. Please don't forget it: 'Once a man of Stobrec, always a man of Stobrec.'"

Nodding and bowing to him, I thank him and go. I will not forget any of it.

My mother died at age eighty-five in September, 2006, with my brother and I at her side, each of us holding one of her hands, in a nursing home in Portland, Oregon. A gifted music thanatologist named Barbara Cabot beautifully sang for us, playing a magnificent, full-sized orchestral harp that helped guide her spirit from her body. My mother was strikingly beautiful even in the terrible moments just before her death. After a period of acute loss and grieving, I began to get on with my life, as I knew I would, now parentless, with a keen awareness of my utter vulnerability on the immediate firing line of life, clinging to my youngest, most sweet, little daughter, not wanting to let go of her.

But since that first afternoon when Nat and I arrived in Split at the Hotel Park, my mother has come rushing back to me in all her girlish charm, in some new delightful guise and dress, refreshed and cleansed, a pure young carefree girl, a young beauty of the Dalmatian coast. I was seeing my mother again as she was or might have been, had she been happy. I now had no choice but to think of her, not just because of Tatiana, but because I kept catching glimpses of my mother as a young woman everywhere I go: walking on the marble flagstones in the September sunshine, shopping in the city market, dining in one of the outdoor restaurants. Split was my mother's city. My mother is everywhere.

Is there a word to describe an entire city of beautiful women? An Exquitopolis? Gorgeousville? One would have to be blind not to consider Split such a place. As we sat in the cafés on the Riva we would watch them walk past, as if on a runway, Dada staring at them the entire length of the promenade, as if encouraging me to stare, too, or at least to invite a comment from me.

"Yes, the women of Split are great beauties," I tell her, as one extraordinary example of Dalmatian womanhood passes by.

"They are famous for it," she says with a nod.

"The way they dress, the colors, they are definitely calling attention to themselves. They want to draw your eye and be admired," I say.

"Well, yes, of course," Dada says, to this remarkably bland and intentionally innocuous comment. "All Croatia's Miss World contestants come from Split. The Elite modeling agency sends a team from Paris here every year to comb the city streets."

Split is a glamor capital. The women of the Dalmatian coast are not shy about showing off in the Adriatic sunshine. They wear evening wear—sequins, heels, big jewelry—at breakfast. They are tall and slender, with bronze skin, and long, straight hair. Some are elegantly dressed, while others favor wildly alluring, eye-catching ensembles. The women of Split have it and they flaunt it.

I don't know if there is a gene for flashy female apparel, but if so, Goldie came by it honestly. As a young man she embarrassed me terribly with her gaudy wardrobe. She never spent any time here, yet she was of this place. When my mother appeared at parent weekend freshman year wearing an outlandish white fur coat, not suitable, I thought, for my new high brow life as an undergraduate, it would have been better for both of us if I knew where she came from. I apologize to you now, mom, for not welcoming you more warmly that day. Now I know you: an exuberant girl from the Dalmatian coast who loved to dress beautifully.

If you have a sexpot for a mother, you should examine her gene pool and village of origin. Perhaps her ancestors, like my mother's, were Mediterranean. Sexpots sprout and grow in the Mediterranean region as healthily as eggplant.

Goldie's extravagant personal style, I thought, betrayed her humble, Chicago, working-class origins, not anything Mediterranean. She claimed to know all Europe, being raised in a European household in a community of Europeans. To me, it appeared, she grew up on the south side of Chicago with a collection of rough-cut Chicagoans. I did not believe that anyone could claim to be European or know Europe if, like my mother, they had spent less that two or three weeks in Europe their entire lifetime. It turns out, I was totally wrong about that, too. That neighborhood in Chicago was nearly as completely European as the original.

Mom and I had other issues. She always expressed strength, not weakness. She was outward, never inward. My history with her was a long process of invalidating my interior life. When I complained about a problem or needed to explore a matter, she'd brush me off with a wave, saying: "I never promised you are rose garden."

Her goal was to toughen me up for life's bumpy road. After a certain age, I stopped discussing anything with her that was complicated or important.

She enthusiastically embraced the mobile, fragmented, modern American definition of family. "Birds gotta fly," she told me cheerfully, as if I really were a bird that had to leave the nest. She made no attempt to keep me near her. As far as she was concerned, the further I moved away from Chicago, the better. "Give them roots and give them wings" was another favorite cliché. Then there was the flower pot. As a family, my mother, father, brother and I were together in one flower pot. As we got older, my brother and I were transplanted into our own pots, she explained, a notion that filled me with sadness. This connected with another expression which she had framed and hung on the kitchen wall: "Bloom where you are planted."

"Bloom where you are planted," as I understood it, exposed my mother's misery with my father and her profound cluelessness about the values and predicament of her life. Bloom where you are planted was the daily pep talk she gave herself. It was a positive message, upbeat. It was how she got through her days.

My poor mom. We were trapped in America. What advice was she going to give me? To move back to Stobrec into an apartment on "The Street of the Fishermen" within hailing distance of Yugoslavian cousins where we could all live in the same flower pot? That blackboard had been wiped clean. There was no going back. Or that's what she thought. In America, we were in a desert on a horse with no name, but it was all OK because dad bought her a new 450SL.

Thanks to Tatiana and her family I was coming to terms with the death of my mother two years after her passing and my orphancy in midlife. With both parents dead, my children gone, and my wife married to her work, there was plenty of emptiness to grieve. How could I have so screwed up my own life to find my wife and children so far from me? And I was terrified that I had mindlessly repeated the same offenses from my own confused parents with the children I loved. My wife's family was no better. They were as fractured and damaged as any. Our families offered us few insights or examples about authentic happiness or how to live.

Dalmatia and the family I found here showed me something I did not know I had. I came here thinking I was alone, possibly for the duration of the time left to me. But I am not alone. I am connected to this place and its people. Deeply connected.

———

The Picaferaj felt like the right choice for dinner, and when I walked in my boys Petar and Ivo looked positively shocked to see me again. I learned something very important that evening: If anyone in a restaurant in Split, Croatia, offers you a dish consisting of monkfish wrapped in prosciutto, go for it. Bathed in fresh olive oil, this was one of the most spectacular dishes I have ever consumed, anywhere at anytime. The presentations are not three star fussy, but the quality of the ingredients is incomparable. Fortunately for all of us, I am not the only client in the restaurant this evening and not the center of attention.

But they do ask me if I have spent much time with my family in Stobrec.

"Yes," I tell them.

"Who are they, what are their names?" little Ivo asks.

"Plosnic. They own the restaurant Epetium in Stobrec."

Ivo considers this and his face brightens with enthusiasm: "You have some very nice relatives!"

"Thank you. Yes," I reply.

"I have been in that restaurant one hundred times," tall Petar says.

Split is a little like Charlottesville. Everyone knows everyone else.

After that first glass of white wine from Korcula, I ask them what the reaction would be if I moved here permanently from the U.S.A. and took up residence in Split. Ivo pauses, then responds, as if from on high, by saying that Split has seen much history, that it is two thousand years old, thereby suggesting that Split has seen insanity to top anything I might devise.

Petar says, with encouragement, that everyone in Split is friendly. "If you could not get home and fell asleep drunk on the sidewalk, no one would steal your wallet. It would still be there in your pocket in the morning," Petar says with enthusiasm. He is obviously referring to the last time I dined with them at the Picaferaj.

The next evening, as planned, I take a cab into Stobrec and let myself out on the waterfront across from the tourism office, and start to walk up Mornarska Street to the restaurant.

On the street, up the hill ahead of me in a gravel parking lot, a cluster of village children are kicking around a soccer ball in the waning minutes of daylight. As I approach this group of small children, a little brown haired girl splits off from the pack and runs straight over to me, dancing, light on her feet. It's Anna, Tatiana's adorable seven year old daughter. She could be Paulina or my mother as a little girl.

I don't know how to greet unsupervised seven year olds anymore in a way that's natural. In America, we have been taught and trained not to touch small children for so many years that we just don't go near them physically any longer, and I don't know what the custom is here. I end up awkwardly tapping her on the top of her head as if she were a dog. But I feel lucky that this little girl recognized me and felt comfortable enough to run over and welcome me. I get down on my knees so that I am almost eye level with her, and she rewards me with a smile. My normal human instinct is to wrap this child up in my arms and kiss her on the cheeks and forehead. Two of her little friends are watching with curiosity from a distance. If upon entering an ancient village and being greeted on the street with a familiar smile by a small child is not a sign of acceptance and belonging, I do not know what is. Little Anna can tell I appreciate her welcome.

The restaurant is quiet this evening; only a few tables are occupied; it's already starting to feel like the end of the season. Darko, dressed for work in a short-sleeved white shirt and navy blue bow tie, looks up from behind the bar and greets me and leads me to a table in the rear, where we just sit together and look at each other without so much as a word. His defensive posture towards me from our original meeting—"Who is he? What does he want?"—is gone. Our brief wordless exchange is as far as the planned encounter between us goes, because, just as he is about to say something, the beautiful Tatiana rushes in with ten year old son Rudy, who fist hits me, along with Dada, who is all dressed up and ready to go. Vlado and the Big Fixer, Dada says, are fetching the car.

While we wait for them to arrive we drink white wine and examine a box of Plosnic family photographs which Dada has brought downstairs from the house. They are all old photographs of Konstantin as a young man which Dada, one by one, holds up to my face for comparison.

"Priest Branko Stepinac told me about these pictures," I say.

"Branko Stepinac! Branko Stepinac! Humph!" Tatiana exclaims with disapproval.

"Tatiana, he is a good man. Give him a chance."

Vlado runs downstairs into the restaurant looking cheerful, rubbing his hands together, and signals that we are ready to leave. He looks me in the eye and presents me the agenda for the evening. We are going to a very nice place, he tells me. It's up in the mountains, about a forty-five-minute drive, and he looks at me to see if this registers, if the plan meets with my approval.

"It's a very nice place," Tatiana tells me. "You will like it."

"That's why I'm here," I nod. "Let's go!"

The little gray car parked in front of the restaurant is about the size of the original Mini Cooper, not the new larger version reintroduced a few years ago. It may be a Fiat, but I cannot tell for sure in the growing darkness. All I know is that this type of car is not a familiar sight on American roads. Vlado is driving and all five of us somehow squeeze in, me in the passenger seat, Dada, Tatiana, and the Big Fixer my cousin all somehow fitted sideways and on top of each other in the back. After a quick stop at a roadside market, we start driving east, climbing away from the sea and up into the mountains. Vlado has the car radio on and Tatiana is singing along in the back seat as if she were a thirteen year old.

When an old traditional song comes on, complete with violins and accordion music, they all instantly stop talking and loudly exhale "aaah." Vlado turns the volume way up, and they all sing in unison. These are the old, much-loved, sentimental songs from their parent's and grandparent's epoch, they are beautiful even without knowing the words, these are the songs with a narrative line about love or sadness and disappointment and heartbreak, and my cousins react to this music like the French respond to Edith Piaf, or Americans react when a great old Sinatra or Billie Holiday tune is played and you hear it again as if for the first time. But no Americans I know would sing along in full voice like this, besides my youngest daughter, who like Tatiana, knows how to have a good time. They'd all be too self-conscious about it. Back home, this conduct would be considered unsophisticated or uncool.

Washington Mutual declared bankruptcy today, September 25th, and when I stole a glance at my computer in my yellow apartment this morning I saw that the Dow had fallen by 600 points. Five thousand miles away from my former office at the Big Firm and my blood ran cold—for a moment or two. No one here in the car with me now mentions this frightening news headline, no one cares, not even the Big Fixer, the successful capitalist in the family. With my knees pressed up against the dashboard of the tiny car, I have one thought only: Thank God I left the Big Firm. I am relieved to be with my Dalmatian kin, right here, right now, out of the poisonous reach of CNBC, CBS, MSNBC, the *Journal*, the *Post*, and the *Times*. I worry for a second about sweet Dalmatia and its burgeoning tourism economy. The Germans, Italians, and French will come as always, but the free-spending American hedge fund managers and financial services attorneys will probably not have Croatia on the top of their travel list next year. But these Croatians have seen a lot worse in their lifetimes than a serious recession and a few seasons of negative growth. They are tough, they are masters of adversity, and they will adapt.

We are driving up into the stony karst of the Dalmatian zagora, a Transylvanian, eastern European landscape the likes of which I have never seen. The Adriatic-Mediterranean-Italianate-Venetian world of the coast has vanished in the blink of an eye. While we are technically still within Dalmatia and Croatia, we have come ever closer to the stark Bosnian frontier and the nighttime landscape is haunting. Croatia is less than twenty-five miles across at this point on the map.

Vlado drives like a lunatic. He propels the stuffed little car around the hairpin turns on two wheels, overtaking a bus belching fumes on a one-hundred-meter straightaway in the face of oncoming traffic moving towards us at high speed. I look back at Tatiana with eyes wide, say "holy shit," and they all laugh at me. I turn and face Vlado and sincerely ask him to please slow down, but he thinks I'm joking. I tell myself to just let go, that I am entering the heart of darkness. If I am going to die tonight I will at least be in the company of newfound family.

The forty-five-minute estimated time of arrival turns into an hour, then an hour and a half. We are driving in rugged mountain valleys, crossing the Cetina River with its rushing white water, with every bleak mountaintop punctuated by the illuminated stone cross of the local church. The succession of illuminated crosses maps our route through the mountains.

Vlado tells me this is wild country, that packs of wolves roam freely at night. I tell them I am certain they are driving me up here to slit my throat, and they laugh wildly at this notion.

The border between Dalmatia and Bosnia, I am discovering, is marked by the main range of the Dinaric Alps which reach altitudes exceeding 7,000 feet. This drive was no casual outing.

Just as we pull up to our destination, a towering stone house at the end of a gravel lane in deep country, which was itself at the termination of two other unpaved and rutted roads, the red fuel warning light on the dashboard comes on. We are almost out of gas. It's 10 P.M.; we are somewhere near the fortified Bosnian border; there are no gas stations, no 7-11's up here. They do not accept VISA or MasterCard.

We step out of the car onto high ground, dry windswept open country far above and beyond the sea, not another house light burning anywhere in any direction, only the blackness of night, not a star in the sky. The night air here is cooler and drier than the moist, salt and sea scented breezes of Split. The sprawling estate where we have landed—the Villa Olka— is the home of Dundo, one of the great forces of nature in the Serbian-Bosnian-Croatian love-hate triangle, a musician of considerable local celebrity, a larger-than-life personality, and a man with an enormous capacity for food, women, fun, and friendship. Dundo is one of those people who can carry it off with just one name. Mention Dundo to any restaurant owner, café manager, or hotel concierge in Split and you get an immediate nod of approval.

This short, powerfully built man greets us at his massive front door by scooping up Tatiana and whirling her around as if she were riding a carousel that's spinning out of control, the two of them howling with laughter. As my eyes become acclimated to the dark, I see that we are standing in the front courtyard of a compound of stone structures, barns, outbuildings, and cottages, all of intriguing sensibility and design, and all newly renovated. Dundo swings open the door with a smile to a brightly lit interior and bids us welcome. He greets Dada with the same effusiveness he displayed for Tatiana, salutes the Big Fixer with the respect a man his stature is due, and cuffs Vlado with a playful punch. To me, he bows in courtly fashion, welcoming me to his abode, which is none too humble. Dundo is barrel chested, with chiseled arms and broad back. Good energy and health radiate from him. He has dark hair that he wears fashionably short, four or five weeks removed from a buzz cut, and a black and gray beard of one or two weeks growth. He is not exactly pristine in his appearance. He is wearing a pair of old gray overhauls and a white short-sleeved shirt, and a worn-out pair of boat shoes. All of his clothes are deeply stained with red wine. Dundo has been making wine all day in his winery, housed in a large room just off the kitchen. Dundo is nonstop action, roving from guest to guest, talking, laughing, filling our glasses.

There are a dozen or more people inside and a dozen or more open bottles of wine standing on the ceremonial dining room table. The decor is modern hunting lodge, with heavy antique armchairs and carved chests of drawers that might furnish a castle, oversized candelabras, modern black leather sofas, glass and wrought iron side tables, armoires full of books, silver wine buckets, wine paraphernalia of all sorts, and flat-screen televisions and video equipment in nearly every room. I have seen mountain mansions like this in Colorado outside Vail and Aspen, but did not expect to come across such a fanciful construction up here so near the fiercest fighting of the last war. This is a hell of a place for a party, a veritable twenty-room man cave, and indeed, Dundo later tells me he is the only divorced person that he knows.

Long-stemmed glass in hand, Dundo leads us on a tour of the property. The original nineteenth century stone farm house Dundo inherited from his father, the massive, sprawling additions are of his own design and construction. There are some nifty engineering feats on display. The swimming pool, with a view of the valley, is built above the sauna, so that while seated in the sauna you can look up to the sky through the thick glass bottom of the pool. Dundo has rigged this pool-sauna complex so that the sauna heats the pool. This system works exactly as designed, and Dundo takes as much delight in it as Willie Wonka.

Around 11 P.M.—the hour in Dalmatia when everyone starts to come alive—we all sit down to a big dinner culminating in a dish of pasta and wild boar, which was shot on a nearby mountainside by one of the guests, an accomplished hunter, and all prepared by Lucia, Dundo's diminutive, sparkling, eighty-four-year-old mother, standing there beaming at us from the beautiful kitchen created by her son. By eighty, I cannot help but think, my mother was out of it on Zoloft, riveted to television installments of Judge Judy, Judge Joe Brown, and other Judge shows from the mechanized bed in her nursing home, with an emergency call button at the ready in the event she needed help getting to the toilet. Mom moved into a nursing home and lived there for fifteen years because that is an American way of dealing with the elderly. Frequently when I'd call she'd tell me it was an inconvenient time to speak, that Judge Judy was on and that she had "a good case," and I'd put the phone down with a sigh.

Lucia lives in this big country house with her son and moves into a tiny apartment in Split during the winter months. Dundo gazes upon his mother with love and affection. She is a critical part of his life, he tells me, she is integrated into her community, she is hugged and kissed by all the guests in thanks for the fine meal she has prepared. Dundo tells me that Lucia stays active, she is not dependent on cars, she goes everywhere on foot, she shops at the city market, she knows what she needs to do to take care of herself. Lucia's eyes twinkle. She is alive and alert.

Each guest in turn walks up and introduces himself to me graciously and with a special word of kindness. They are men and women, from Serbia, Bosnia, Croatia, and Dalmatia, even one Slovenian. This high-octane, combustible cocktail of races and religions freezes me because I know the terrible history of the region. I had no idea the various ethnic groups interacted, much less partied together on Friday nights. All the warring parties of the 1990's have assembled this evening in Dundo's dining room, and I think the place could go up like tinder. When I see how much wine they are consuming, and how effortlessly they are laughing, I decide to calm myself down. This spread of political persuasions would be unimaginable at my house. Social life as I know it, certainly as it exists in my hometown, is not so multifaceted. The hunter neighbor is dressed in a suede olive-green tunic, a classic Bavarian costume, as if he stepped from the Gorsuch catalog. There are two dark and lively Serbian sisters with their Croatian husbands who live across the border in Bosnia and sing backup for Dundo's ensemble. They tell me they are performing at a wedding in Bosnia next weekend, and they invite me to join them. Then there is also Sasha and Layla, Dada's Bosnian-Dutch son and Bosnian daughter in law.

By the end of the evening all of them are gently teasing me, calling me "Plosnic." As in: "Plosnic, is the wine to your taste?" Or: "Plosnic, there is a little house for sale in the village that is perfectly suited for you." I felt flattered and loved by them.

In tête-à-têtes, Tatiana has shared the story of the surprise appearance of Nat and I at her home, and they look up and smile at me both shyly and knowingly. They are all curious to hear me tell it, in my own words. A polite hush comes over the table when I start in, and I tell the story of meeting them as simply as I am able.

Discovering Tatiana and her father is one of the remarkable events of my life, I say. If I had known them forever, I would be far the richer for it. To be acknowledged and welcomed by them as one of their own is a gift I will never forget, one of the greatest kindnesses I have ever been offered. A part of me I never knew has sprung alive here in this beautiful land of my Dalmatian past. I am someone who always put the needs of my family first, ahead of my own, and I was happy to do so because I loved them, and today I am an adoring father and husband.

But now I am shedding old skin and hoping for renewal, I tell them. I want to discover the magic of living again before I get sick or die. Now was the time for me to live well before it is too late, and I am honored to be with them, connecting with them, beginning this process in their company.

Halfway through this spiel I recognize I'm totally invested in its outcome, praying I get through, that I strike a chord, that they accept my words, and the applause and smiles of appreciation around the table melts me with happiness. My speech is meaningful to them. Everyone in the room chimes in with anecdotes of their own. They understand how a man with as much gray as brown in his hair has found his way to Dalmatia, turning up unannounced at Tatiana's front door. They take pleasure in my tale of family reconnection after so much history, the remarkable evidence of Paulina's birth certificate, and the corroboration of the village priest. Their faces are full of comprehension and warmth. They are more than commonly polite, as a group, but they may also be genuinely moved by this tale. I am pleased that they do not consider me a disconnected man, a lost soul wandering the earth.

They also tell me, with the ultimate of courtesy that makes me shake my head in wonder, that it was a tragic loss for the nation of Croatia and the land of Dalmatia that I had not been born there and lived my life among them. The elegance and gallantry of this sentiment overwhelms me.

It strikes me sharply, in the next second, that no group of Americans, no relatives or acquaintances of mine, if gathered on my porch in Virginia for an evening to welcome distant cousins from southern Europe, if this situation were reversed, would regard visitors from foreign places with such genuine kindness and interest as I was welcomed that evening at Dundo's home. I felt honored by their attention to me and shamed knowing I came from a place that was too self-absorbed to return the favor.

I also say to the party gathered around Dundo's dining room table that it is a universal desire to know where you come from. This statement has less resonance because all of them know precisely where they come from, a thorough understanding of their ancestry and the names and dates on their family tree. I am the one who lost touch with his personal history, not them. They could not imagine not knowing where they come from. In Tatiana's case, she comes from a village once called Epetium, where her 10th great grandmother walked along the same Adriatic shore her daughter Anna walks today. Her story may be as old as that of Diocletian and the late emperors of Rome. Tatiana also knows that Anna's granddaughter will walk the beach in Stobrec, too, that people named Plosnic will live in Stobrec as long as the family and the village endure. For so many, there isn't this certainty in America.

"I have always lived for myself, I have always put myself first," the Big Fixer says to me with a shrug. Although his is not quite so simple a story. He has an adult daughter he adores, who has married a Croatian. They emigrated to Australia, and he loves his daughter and son-in-law enormously.

"If you do not do it for yourself, no one else will," Sasha chimes in.

"It's time to live. Don't put it off. Time is short. Move fast," one of the Serbian vocalists interjects, full of animation.

These are Europeans. They are already sold on carpe diem.

Dundo is a Serb living in Dalmatia. He had a distinguished career as a maritime architect and worked in New Zealand for many years. He has gladly hung it up.

"I am a gypsy," he explains to us gathered around the table, throwing his hands in the air. "I have to be me." Dundo is now playing music all over southern Europe and has recorded ten discs of original compositions. The man loves life.

"Who did you think I was when I first knocked on your door?" I ask Tatiana.

"I thought you were lost tourists looking for a sobe," she answers. "We get them in Stobrec from time to time."

General conversation takes over, extremely animated, even boisterous, not a single word about politics, some interest in the subject of Croatia entering the European Union but only lukewarm. Dundo says he will produce nine hundred liters of wine this year in his winery off the kitchen, enough for his family and friends, but EU rules would shut down his home operation. Somehow I repeat the same stupid remark about the trash dumps on Korcula, Brac, and Hvar, and Layla instantly gets testy about it. They complain about the corruption, a problem in all of ex-Yugoslavia. Everyone is drinking the red wine, the white wine, the rosé, and the plum brandy, everyone except good old Vlado, I am happy to see, who has sacrificed his pleasure this evening as the designated driver. None of the Plosnics smoke cigarettes, including me, but everyone else is puffing away. Lucia bids us all a fond goodnight and goes upstairs to bed, our thanks for the excellent meal resounding around the room.

Dundo plays for us his latest music video, in which he stars, along with his handsome son. The music is of the type we heard on the radio driving up the mountain—a sentimental heart felt song between a father and his son about their stormy but loving relationship, a beautiful duet. We cheer when it concludes and Dundo looks gratified.

There is much knowledgeable wine talk. Everyone present makes their own wine, speaks at length about their procedures, their favorite grapes and wine regions, what local wine recently won what medal, but if there was a consensus favorite among the best products from this ancient wine civilization, it would be the white wines of Slovenia. The world's best wines outside the Mediterranean zone, according to this sophisticated group, come from Australia, New Zealand, and Chile, but they really don't care a whit for any non-local wine and do not drink it, and would not buy it even if available for purchase. No one in the room has even the smallest interest in the Napa Valley, but the Big Fixer has met famous Dalmatian-born Mike Grgich, winner of the so-called "Judgement of Paris" and the owner of Grgich Hills in Rutherford, California. He also knows the Babich family, native Dalmatians who are now among the important wine producers of New Zealand. He concedes that he would be interested in tasting their wines, but his life does not depend upon it. The Slovenian wines and the homegrown Dalmatian wines suit him just fine.

It's nearly 3 A.M. when Tatiana asks me across the table: what do I want to do now, return to Split or spend the night at Dundo's castle? She asks in a neutral voice, as if it is completely up to me. I say: Tatiana, it is your call, whatever you decide is all right with me. We talk at length about the fact that car's fuel warning light has lit up, and Sasha teases us that if we leave and head back to Split and run out of gas, that they could not rescue us because there is no cell reception anywhere on that mountain road, that we will end up sleeping in the car or attacked by wolves when we get out of the car to take a leak. Tatiana and Vlado consider their three children to pack off to school that morning. I am confident about Vlado's physical state. While everyone else is tipsy, he is sober and clear-eyed.

We decide to drive home and risk the wolf attack. Vlado knows the car; he trusts it can make it back to Split without running out of gas. I ask, tipsy myself: Vlado, are you sure

about this? Are you certain? I would rather accept Dundo's
hospitality than run out of gas on that road in the middle of
the night.

"We can make it. Yes, I'm certain." Driving off feels like a
huge gamble.

As we prepare to go, Dundo asks about my departure from
Dalmatia to return home, and I tell him I have a few days
more. "Good," he says, "I have a place near Split I want to
show you."

We all pile back into the tiny gray badgeless car, except
for my cousin the Big Fixer who is by now asleep upstairs
in one of the distant bedrooms. As soon as Vlado turns the
ignition switch, the red fuel warning light flashes on. This will
be interesting.

Vlado drives down the mountain, if possible, at an even
higher rate of speed than the drive up. We encounter not a
single vehicle on the dark road to impede us. Vlado has his
left hand attached to the high beam yoke for the entire drive,
rapidly flashing his bright lights on and off well in advance of
every hairpin turn in order to alert any drunk driver heading
in our direction. I have never seen anyone drive a car at night
in this fashion. Tatiana assures me repeatedly in a groggy voice
that Vlado is an excellent driver, and indeed, he is. Dada is
asleep in the back. I'm holding on as we spin around the turns.
We are tumbling down the arid mountainside towards sea level
like a Formula I car on course for victory.

We finally see the first few city lights, then the wide, flat
coastal road that leads into Split, and then, just ahead of us,

the only gas station in the entire city that is open 24 hours. When Vlado sees it, he releases an audible sigh and we laugh. Somehow he drove us down the mountain for forty-five minutes with the red fuel warning light on. He and Tatiana confer among themselves, collect some kuna between them, and pay for less than half a tank of petrol. Then Vlado gets back in and drives me into the city center, letting me off at the taxi stand about three blocks from the pedestrian zone where I live. I don't know how they are going to be feeling when they have to get their kids going for school in a couple of hours.

It's 4 A.M and the streets are empty and dark save for all the city's packs of colorful feral cats wandering around, crying at me as I pass, poking through the garbage with their tiny paws. One of the outdoor cafés in the square is being washed down by a man with a power hose who does a double take when he sees me. I let myself in at 6 Tonciveva Street, and go upstairs to sleep.

Six

DALMATIA REPUBLICA

My journey to Dalmatia, begun as a father-son bicycle trip with an ancillary ancestry hunt haphazardly attached, was now turning a lifetime of prejudice and misinformation on its ass about first and second-world countries, and I now felt quite certain that the U.S.A. is the impoverished culture, not Croatia. It was me, not my backward Croatian cousins, as my mother and Dorothy surmised in 1966, who came from underprivileged circumstances. I was feeling like I had been exported to sane Dalmatia after a lifetime inside one of the big photographs in the "Spiritual America" series by Richard Prince—random skid marks, advertising images, landscapes of cowboys, biker chicks, and grotesque celebrities. At the moment, America wasn't comparing well with little Dalmatia in any category. All the food in Dalmatia is local and organic, university tuition is $1,000 per year, and health care is a body of wisdom passed from one generation to the next. I saw a Vienna-educated physician in Split for an upset stomach, who examined me, told me to cut back on coffee, and charged me twenty kuna (less than $4) for the visit. When you sit down for lunch with friends in America, after discussing the wars in Iraq and Afghanistan, homeland security, the cost of health insurance, the shattered economy, and how to pay your kid's way through college, all the fun has left the building.

In any case, I am glad to be here and not there. I am not sure what *there* represents any longer. *Here*, I am starting to understand and deeply appreciate. I only know that I want to remain here and not return there anytime soon. And why, with only personal uncertainty facing me, would I ever want to go back?

I can breathe again. I have not tired of Dalmatia and have not longed for home, only more mystified how my home has become so aberrant and cheerless, how we have so much more than them but so much less. I am not curious about anything going on there, nothing in the news, nothing in sports, nothing from my friends, some of whom, I can only assume, are suffering from the financial meltdown, as I would be too if I were with them in the narrow groove of my old life or paying attention to the news. I don't yearn to hear American voices, see American faces, or learn American opinions. I can spend an entire morning in a café not networking with anyone. I don't miss the experience of driving my car to a shopping mall, then getting back in the car to drive to a different store at the far end of the same mall because it's too far or too boring to walk. I am not sure how, having broken through, if or in what capacity I can go back. I do know that going back the same person isn't a possibility.

Every morning, with the big bathroom windows open to the humming city square below, I find myself singing in the shower. The tiny seed of an inspiration takes root. I could live like this: in an apartment above a café, in a city, without a car. I begin to design a life for myself that is smaller and more humble, not a big life to brag about, but a real life to live. If only there was someone out there I could persuade to live it with me.

I recall what Lawrence Durrell wrote about the Adriatic, "What more does a man want than an olive tree, a native land, and woman from his own place?"

With a week remaining in Split, my days take on a sweet routine of their own, and for the entire week I do not leave the city limits. I do not go to Trogir, Zadar, or gorgeous Opatija in Istria as I thought I might. Instead, I meet sunny Tatiana, "enjoying her as she was, taking her as she was," as Durrell wrote of Justine, accompanied by an ever changing configuration of family and friends, at the same big café on the Riva at about ten every brilliant morning, where I join in the talk about aged aunties, the foibles and life history of the beloved Konstantin, the quality of the recently completed grape harvest, the trials and tribulations of our teenage children. And I walk along the white marble streets to go swimming at Bacvice every afternoon for an hour or so of relaxation, decompression, casual observation of city life, and immersion in the baptismal waters of my ancestors, and I feel them around me, reviving my skin and rejuvenating my spirit. A minute in the Adriatic cures whatever ails me.

In a wonderful bookstore in the thick of Diocletian's Palace, I buy the imposing, 1,200-page Penguin edition of the history of Yugoslavia, *Black Lamb and Grey Falcon*, published in 1938, and develop a profound appreciation for the mind of Rebecca West. This book, in the edition I purchase, is dedicated by the author "to my friends in Yugoslavia who are now all dead or enslaved." It is realistic to speculate that I might not be here today if my four grandparents did not flee Europe when they did, if they had not sensed the dangerous gathering storms in Europe, and had not America opened its doors to them and millions of others. Europe became caught up in a thirty-year maelstrom of hate. My grandparents got out just in time, for the sake of themselves, my parents, me, my children, and my precious new granddaughter born into the world in Sacramento, California.

Bozo my landlord acknowledges me with a smart salute in the public squares of Split. Any man with the power to instruct a cash machine to spew out 100 kuna banknotes as easily as I is worthy of formal greeting. He tells me he has the perfect apartment for me next year when I return with my family, in the same building, but a larger unit. I shop in the city market every morning and experience that chemistry with the vendors—the lightening quick calculation, the narrowing of the eyes, the instantaneous appraisal of the giveaway signs I am not a native of Split, something about my shirt, my teeth, my hair, or my ease, and the price quickly escalates twenty percent. I pay. Wandering around the fish market and the food stalls, browsing in the bookshops, walking everywhere, exploring every remote back street and nook-and-cranny in stony Split, stepping inside its tiny neighborhood churches, taking photographs, preparing simple meals for myself, sitting downstairs reading in the café with its hyper-Western atmosphere of chain smoking, cell phone-addled teenagers, and relentless pounding techno music—these are glorious days. Cigarettes are still mandatory fashion accessories among the young and the techno music will drive you crazy, but at least the kids are connecting with one another.

Back home at Shenandoah Joe's, my favorite coffee spot in Charlottesville, the café denizens are huddled over their titanium-encased laptops, faces bathed in the glow of their monitors. No one is speaking to each other with any animation at Shenandoah Joe's; they whisper, like in church or the graduate student lounge. If you express a casual pleasantry to someone it's akin to an intrusion, like rousing them from a stupor. The café population in Charlottesville sit perfectly still; many wear headphones. No one is rustling the pages of a newspaper because people don't read newspapers any longer. There may be two or three people who are networking after organizing a meeting on Facebook, but otherwise, my local coffee shop is quiet, save for the rapping of fingers on keyboards, the hiss of the expresso machine, and the refrain of the barista, repeated without variation to each person in line: "Do you want room for cream?" On the bulletin board at Shenandoah Joe's someone put up a flyer advertising "Laughter Class."

As my days wind down, it strikes me that I want to meet other cousins in the village, but not if it means I have to take

time away from Tatiana, who has reshuffled her life during my
visit. There are ten Plosnic households in Stobrec, and I have
only interacted with the family of Konstantin, met the Big
Fixer, and shook hands with the Plosnic woman from the tall
stone house across the street. I haven't examined the Blazevich
side, nor have I traveled up into the mountains to the village of
Bisko, as Nat and I originally intended, where my grandfather,
Paulina's husband, was born, and where, God knows, families
named Simundza might still be living, and where I might
yet stare into the face of my long-deceased grandfather. The
Plosnics are masters of the Adriatic Sea, bronze-skinned
fishermen, ship builders, musicians, and wine makers. The
upland Simundzas are men of stone, tall, chiseled, of great
physical strength, ruminative and deliberate, more Slavic in
their features, and no strangers to a good fight, I would guess.
My mother's brother, my uncle Jerry, was the boxing champion
in his U.S. Army unit in the Pacific during World War II, and
he inherited that skill from his Simundza father, not from his
diminutive mother, Paulina Plosnic. But the female principle
rules. I am captivated by one Plosnic woman in particular who
has brought my mother back to life. The Simundza men will
have to wait.

Also, I don't want Tatiana and Vlado to think I'm leaving
them after all their kindness to me. Somehow, I have a
profound sense of guilt with them, accepting their hospitality
while having forsaken them, dropping them from the dance
card, back in 1913, and not wanting to leave them again.

I can understand and forgive my parents for their actions concerning the old country. I knew no Dalmatians growing up or anyone with any interest in visiting their country of origin. Only the most creative and unorthodox parent would have dreamt of taking their children from America to Split for spring break in 1969, although many Italian Americans I know make a habit of going back to their Italian families every year, knowing more than the basics about the Italian language and civilization, and sometimes staying for months on end. Like everyone else that year in our neighborhood on the North Shore of Chicago, we went to Palm Springs or Acapulco or San Juan, far less interesting, but more fashionable destinations for Chicagoans of the late 1960's.

At moments, I worry that this trip is only about the past, what went before, that it's too late for me, that I am in permanent exile, that I'll always remain on the periphery with no reasonable hope of lasting reattachment. The language is too difficult. I express my most powerful, personal thoughts to them in English, and they understand, but it would take years to speak Croatian with fluency. For my Dalmatian relatives, the village of Stobrec is their centerpoint, as it has been for generations. They complain about each other but they have each other in a way we do not. It is I who am the pawn of world history, as I see it now, washed by the tides of warfare and suffering on a ship of immigrants, bound for America, born on the south side of Chicago, thousands of miles from my ancestral home.

Now that I have found them, how can we stay meaningfully attached? Do I buy a bolt-hole in Split? Bring my adult children here on holiday? Invite Konstantin and Tatiana to visit me in America? Or will our important reconnection gradually dissolve into the periodic email or card at Christmas? I would dread that.

For my Dalmatian family, my home in America is terra incognita, unsafe, undesirable, a sequence of ghastly news headlines. They long ago lost sympathy for America, and contact with their American kin, like me, who disappeared into the ether of world events. For permanent residency, Australia and New Zealand are considered more desirable choices for Croatians who want to make a new life. America does not come up on their radar screen as an option for living, working, or visiting. America now is the place where they have an 87 year old relative who is acting like a belligerent asshole. They want to go to the U.S.A. about as much as I want to go to Somalia.

This is baseline. I am back to baseline. I'm there and I'm breathing the air.

I come from a place where people do everything for themselves, and they do all of it together, as a team. They grow their own grapes and olives and make their own wine, brandy, and olive oil. They catch fish from the sea from wooden boats they've built and grow herbs and vegetables in their stony terraced gardens. They provide health care to elderly friends and relatives in their village. They sing and play music together. When called upon, they fiercely defend themselves from enemies, and look to no one else to fight for them. They build beautiful houses of stone and know how to repair them. They may not be rich, but they are not impoverished in their hearts. They know how to live well, in the moment, for today. They party with the best of them. When they hit a wall and can't resolve a difficult issue to their satisfaction, they shrug, say "that's life," accept the sadness, and move on.

Tatiana and her friends know that Tuesday is my day of departure from Split. She tells me that Monday Dundo wants to organize a farewell party for me, to play bocce, at a place dear to Dundo's heart just outside Split, not far from the Riva, just past the Mestrovic museum in the lovely wooded Marjan peninsula, she indicates the general direction with a wave of her hand. It's a very cool place, Tatiana says with enthusiasm. Would the idea of playing bocce with them engage my interest? She takes care to spell out the plan in detail, just as Vlado described the drive up into the mountains to Dundo's distant lair.

Two Italian-American friends of mine in Charlottesville built bocce courts at their homes and I have played bocce with them at least a dozen times. Bocce is a tremendous game with a glass of wine in your hand. The last time I walked through the English Garden in Munich with Nat, there had to be at least thirty bocce games in progress, but the Germans were holding large steins of beer.

"Tatiana, I would love to play bocce with you and Dundo and anyone else who wishes to play, but I warn you I am a very competitive player, my natural athletic ability emerges when

I play bocce, and I may embarrass the other players given the fact that my skill is so exceptional."

Tatiana laughs at my goofy comments, bending forward at the waist as is her habit. We all agree to meet Monday, same time, same place.

Walking back through the crowds to my beautiful orange apartment building at 6 Tonciceva Street, I realize that during my entire three weeks in Split I have only spent two days alone.

Monday morning arrives, September 29, 2008. The United States House of Representatives has opted to play politics with an uncertain economy and today votes to reject a government emergency bailout plan, with the result that the Dow Jones Industrial Average has fallen, today alone, by 777 points, a new record single-day loss. I glean this fact from a quick sneak at my stupid laptop, another impulse move I immediately regret. The news is sickening.

For the thousandth time, I know how lucky I am to be in the full thrall of the Mediterranean morning, walking towards my rendezvous on the public stage of Split, awaiting collection on the Riva by Dalmatian friends who over the course of a few short weeks have shown care and opened their hearts to me, have taken me everywhere with them, and revealed everything there is to know about their families and their lives in Dalmatia. And now they are hosting a sendoff I will always remember.

At my desk today at the Big Firm I'd be dreading every call, watching my net worth and that of my clients drop like a stone, pulling my hair out, on the phone with my doctor for more and stronger beta blockers. Instead, I am walking in the sunlight towards the Adriatic Sea in Split, going to a party where I will eat, drink, and play bocce, on a Monday morning no less, with members of a resilient tribe who know better than to fear and worry.

For a change, I am the first to arrive on the Riva, pleased not to keep anyone waiting. Vlado, Tatiana, and Dada pull up fifteen minutes later in their small, super-fast, fuel-efficient automobile, recognizable in the light of day as a Croatian edition Fiat hatchback. Dundo arrives just seconds behind them, looking stylish, riding a black Vespa scooter with a black helmet. Dundo is going to lead us onwards to the party venue. When I see Dundo, I begin to think: party time. Dundo putt-putts away from the Riva on the Vespa and we head off in pursuit, up into the wooded Marjan, past the Mestrovic museum, past the home of Goran Ivanisevic, and then past the magnificent Vila Dalmacija, directly overlooking the sea, Tito's grand former summer residence, displaying obvious signs of neglect and disrepair. Dundo tells my cousin Tatiana later that he is sure my home in America is easily the size of the Vila Dalmacija. He also suggests that I buy the Vila Dalmacija and keep it as my new summer place in Split. Dundo is thinking that I may be a man of means, and I say nothing to dissuade him of it, though the ongoing financial debacle in America has already cut the value of my investments by at least thirty percent. For his part, Dundo is shaping up as an excellent marker for me, how I could evolve and live an independent and creative life. In any case, Dundo and I are interested in each other, see ourselves as kindred spirits, and are quickly becoming real friends.

Less than one kilometer along the sea road past the Mestrovic museum, Dundo finds a flat grassy spot and pulls the Vespa over and parks. We stop behind him, get out of the car, and start walking on a pathway worn in the grass straight up the hill into a hidden garden. This garden leads to another, and then to a third. These are not so much private gardens as they are large allotments of community garden space, and there are dozens of plots in this area, all highly cultivated. By the time we pass through four such properties, we arrive at our destination, behind a secret wall overgrown with vines and through an arched metal gate. Several people are already here to greet us, including my demonstrative cousin the Big Fixer of Stobrec, some people I am meeting for the first time and whose names I would never learn, a good-natured man with gray hair who appears to be the chef and major domo of this rural retreat, and his wife, a beautiful blond, who is chain smoking. Dada's children are here, plus another big Croatian guy wearing his baseball cap backwards, who tells me: "If it is something we can do tomorrow, we wait until tomorrow," and immediately, I like him. I have brought two bottles of wine, a red and a white, which Dundo accepts with gratitude. This is Dundo's party. Once more, he is our host.

This little green paradise is a walled and leafy bower, with several large shade trees, a roughhewn cottage of bleached white stone, typically Dalmatian, reminiscent of a romantic Lake District hideaway from a poem by Wordsworth, and a large, partially enclosed outdoor dining area with a laid stone terrace. In a corner of the property stands a massive cooking grill built of the identical stone, with red clay tile roof, and a tall brick chimney. This enormous grill is nearly half the size of the little house, and the wood fires are already well stoked and roaring when we arrive. The place is a mini-country estate, entirely self-sufficient, every inch of it groomed and cultivated, thickly planted with rows of ripe lemon, lime, and orange trees; luscious fig trees weighted down with heavy fruit; silver-leafed olive trees; rows of fresh vegetables; huge pink pomegranate; grapes; and an entire fenced-off area for animals: chickens, rabbits, a pair of large turkey, and pigeons. Along the entire length of the property is the raked and well-worn gravel bocce court, approximately regulation size, but with certain quirks and inconsistencies to it, an uphill-downhill slope, and one corner blocked by a piece of wood, so some local knowledge was going to be essential for success. From this elevated position in the hills of the Marjan, the only sound are waves crashing on the Adriatic shore, two or three hundred meters back down the hill.

Sitting, absorbing this small, methodically constructed world, I think of my own city garden in Charlottesville, which may be ten or twelve times the size, beautifully landscaped in its traditional Virginia style with lawns, old azaleas, boxwood, dogwood, magnolias, cedar, and tall white pines, but unproductive, with just a small garden patch. It is nothing compared to the variety of this worked and cultivated plot, with every inch of it, save for the bocce court and flower bed, dedicated to producing something good to eat. While I am blowing leaves, trimming hedges and cleaning gutters, my cousins are harvesting oranges, lemons, grapes and olives. This place is part summer getaway, part Dalmatian country club, relaxed and humble. It is testimony to the high civilization of Dalmatia and I love it here. We arrive just before 11 A.M. and the wine is already flowing.

Our party of eleven settles down to the big wooden table under the arbor. We are going to eat and drink, and the eating and drinking are going to be extraordinary. White wine in green bottles without labels is opened with a bottle opener, and is served, in the traditional Dalmatian fashion, with ice cubes and spring water. Drinking wine with water gives you the staying power to drink wine the entire day, and that's precisely what happens here on the Marjan between games of bocce, we drink throughout the day, I don't know how many bottles we consume, and everyone relaxes, laughs, sings, and tells stories, but no one gets drunk.

The feast is a feast of the greatest magnitude, not to be surpassed by the feasting in any European nation at any time in human history. We are embarking upon what the French call "la grand bouffe." We start with fresh mussels grilled in olive oil and bread crumbs, and we mop up the sauce with fresh baked bread. The mussels are followed by a thousand delicious sardines, unlike any nauseating, slimy sardine ever viewed in America, grilled in olive oil to a light crispy brown. Next to come is succulent tuna, fresh from the sea, two green salads, and a bowl of fresh chick peas. Olive oil is in every crevice of my hands, my lips, my clothing. I am bathing in olive oil.

Then, absolutely without warning, the gray-haired chef, seated at the head of the table, rises to his feet, sticks out his barrel chest, and starts to sing. He sings well and he sings from the heart. Dundo, Vlado, and the Big Fixer know the song he is singing, and they all join in. It's one of those old sweet songs, operatic in quality, with a narrative line. At the end of the song, they all cheer madly and applaud.

"What's going on?" I ask Vlado. "What's this all about?

"He feels good, that's why he is singing," Vlado tells me.

So these Dalmatian men break out in song because (1) They feel good, (2) They like to sing, and (3) They like to sing together.

Quite the change from the crowd at Shenandoah Joe's.

Dundo tells me that the chef is a performer with the professional opera company in Split. Then Dundo stands, links my arm in his, makes me stand up alongside him, and he starts to sing a song that even I can understand. It's an old song about Dalmatia, the mother of all Croatia, and the song consists of the same two words sung endlessly over and over again, "Dalmatia Republica, Dalmatia Republica." It's a song about their home and their families, and it's sung with passion, pride, and love. Even someone like me with no Croatian language skills can understand it. "Dalmatia Republica, Dalmatia Republica."

My story of reconnection with Tatiana and her father is repeated to these newcomers, and my physical features are again closely examined and discussed in detail. For some it is the shape of my face, for some it's my hair, for some it's my skin, but the consensus is: I am pure Dalmatian. I am one of them. They have opened wide the portals of their nationhood to me, they have enacted before me the traditions of their tribe without self-consciousness, and they have let me in.

Playing bocce in Split is competitive. Your opponents cheer when you screw up. They say "thank you" when you make an errant toss. They are taunting, celebrating, chest bumping, high five-ing. The men walk solemnly with their hands behind their backs, arguing, measuring the distance from their balls to the pallino when in doubt. The Big Fixer plays barefoot, with his blue jeans rolled up to mid calf. He's got a deft touch. Dundo is also a proficient player. I do the "tree pose" for internal balance before I take my shot, and the Big Fixer says my style is better than my substance.

We complete game one and sit down for another course of mussels, sardines, tuna, and chick peas, and we are all hungry again.

No one wants to discuss any serious subject. I want to ask how their families survived World War II but no one wants to talk about it. Yet again, I see this is all me. Mine is the typical American inquiry. How did you survive the Communists?

Tell me about the Yugoslavia wars of the 1990s. How did you suffer? How grim were the expressions on the faces of the Nazis when they rolled into Stobrec in 1944?

My kin does not care to relive questions of survival and suffering. They want to live and have fun while there is living and having fun to be had. Questions of survival and suffering may well yet lurk on the horizon. I am the innocent fortunate enough to be born in the midwest during the Eisenhower administration. When I ask about pain and suffering I want them to tell me what it was like, what I missed, and from their reaction I can tell that I did not miss anything good.

I announce that I don't want to leave Dalmatia, and I can see from their faces that they don't hear this a lot. Dundo, who knows what I am doing, who senses where I am in life, who left a conventional career himself, tells me that I need a wife in Dalmatia and a wife in America. Laughing, the other men agree. One says I need to learn Croatian so we can discuss subjects like this in detail.

Then the big guy in the baseball cap suddenly starts to sing an old song, and he sings it well, and two beats into it and they are all singing along loudly. These men break out into cheers and toasts. Simply because they feel good. It makes perfect sense.

Several times during the day, Tatiana comes and goes from the little compound. While we party, she has work to do, basic duties, her mother, her father, her kids, the restaurant, several little old ladies in Stobrec to look after. She comes and goes without complaint. This is her life. We pay five or six thousand dollars a month to keep our elderly parents in nursing homes, and many of us are glad to do so to get them out of our hair, convincing ourselves that they like it there, or somehow they are better off. But my Dalmatian cousins do not have to accumulate a nest egg of one million dollars or more for their future warehouse costs because they know their children, their nieces, nephews, and other children in the village, will look after them. Who is going to take care of Tatiana when she is an old woman? Little Anna, age 7. And Anna will know the drill because she watched her mother at work. This system has another benefit: If you know your children are going to take care of you when you are old, then you are going to take good care of them when they are young.

While dining on the fish and shellfish and laughing and singing with these buoyant extroverts, I cannot help but think that back in the U.S.A. congress is waging political war over the bailout package and the market is going to hell. Looking at my hosts, I don't care. I'm so satisfied. It's Monday and we are singing, drinking, and feasting. Dundo has now unveiled a bottle of homemade brandy.

We rake and drag the uphill-downhill bocce court and play again. Game two has a better outcome. My team beats the Big Fixer's and I get to gently taunt him back. He responds by hugging me and kissing my face.

Dundo's neighbor from the mountains, the famous hunter who favors Tyrolean attire, has supplied us with several dozen freshly shot game birds, which Dada has plucked and cleaned, and which the chef has on the wood grill.

Dada then picks huge green figs from the trees overhanging the bocce court. The chef slices the fat ripe figs and grills them together with fresh mozzarella, passing them around the table. This simple dish might be the gastronomic highlight of my entire month in Dalmatia.

More people arrive, then more bocce, then back to drinking. This day, we are inside a poem by Andrew Marvell:

> What wondrous life is this I lead!
> Ripe apples drop about my head;
> The luscious clusters of the vine
> Upon my mouth do crush their wine;
> The nectarine and curious peach
> Into my hands themselves do reach;
> Stumbling on melons, as I pass,
> Ensnared with flowers, I fall on grass.

Hours after our arrival, deep into the afternoon of my last day in Dalmatia, Konstantin, Tatiana's father, who I have not seen since that first morning when Nat and I knocked on his front door, walks through the garden gate with an easy smile on his face, accompanied by a man in whom I instantly recognize myself. Konstantin walks directly over to me and grips my shoulders with his enormous hands. He wants me to meet his cousin, Matko, whose name I recognize as the author of the recently published *History of Stobrec*. Matko carries with him a beige folder filled with documents. He speaks English flawlessly. He tells me that he has looked forward to meeting me, that Konstantin has shared with him the story of my search for family, that he has made a long study of local history and genealogy, and that he is, in fact, my closest living relative in all Dalmatia.

Matko's face is like looking into a funhouse mirror with all my features jumbled or askew. It's disorienting to see myself so astonishingly replicated, so similar and yet so different. All of our facial features are virtually identical, if viewed in isolation, the wave of our hair, the shape of our mouths, the size and shape of our ears, the golden hue of our skin, but the whole has been reassembled in an entirely different manner. His hair has no gray in it, he wears eye glasses and I do not, he has a flat belly from his olive oil diet whereas I have a protuberance from a lifetime of too much butter. Otherwise, this man is me. His appearance has shocked me as greatly as that first glimpse of Tatiana when she opened her father's front door in Stobrec.

Dundo is quickly looking from my face to Matko's, and back again. He starts laughing, holding his sides. The Big Fixer is silent, taking it all in. Konstantin only smiles.

More stunning, Matko is my exact age, he just four months older than I. We can share stories from high school, university, and our love life framed by the same time line. Matko lives on Mornarska Street within a stone's throw of Konstantin and next door to the village church. And he has come here today to validate and authenticate my history and heritage, to fill in the blanks of my family tree. At this moment, he knows more about me than I do. Right now, he is the most important person in my life.

Matko's Version

Matko has important information to convey and we gather around the wooden table with its sheen of olive oil. He has a scholarly method; he is more interested in facts than emotions, and he has a dry, somewhat academic delivery. This is good, because no one could be more emotional about the subject than I. His sheaf of documents contain a history of our family in Stobrec going back as far as can be authenticated, many old photographs of my grandmother's birthplace in the village, and a history of the house itself.

First, he says with a smile, taking a deep breath, there are Plosnics and then there are Plosnics, and not everyone gets along. This is natural, after many hundreds of years of residence on the same small peninsula. I understand this, not at all fond of one particular neighbor who lives just around the corner from me. Then, he says, no two people anywhere in Dalmatia or Croatia, let alone the former Yugoslavia, agree on the essential facts of the most straightforward historic or contemporary event. No two people will tell you the same story, or recite the facts, in the same way. He is going to present me with his version of family history, based upon his years of research. I understand and accept this, as well.

At bottom, he tells me, looking me in the eye, I come, as far as the Plosnics of Stobrec are concerned, from an extinct line. As far as they are concerned, when I appeared here with my son this September, I came back from the dead. They are as amazed and stunned to meet me as I am to meet them. I am a ghost from the forgotten past, an unexpected visitor, to put it mildly, a veritable apparition. The last person from my family line to reside in Stobrec was my grandmother's sister, my so-called Teta Tereza, who died, unmarried and childless, in a stone house on Mornarska Street in 1970. Another miracle: both Konstantin and Matko knew Tereza and remember her as a good and kind person who worked in the fields and looked after local children.

My grandmother and her seven siblings were all born in the village. Three of them emigrated to the United States and were heard from no more. One died as a two year old. One died in Italy. Two just disappeared. Only Tereza remained in Stobrec, dying at age 86. As far as they were concerned, that was that, we were no more.

To differentiate this line from the many other Plosnic family lines in the long history of the village, according to Matko, it is identified in village lore as the "Vusic" line, and my grandmother's birthplace, her beautiful stone cottage above the sea, is still known in town today as the "Vusic house." Vusic was the maiden name of my great, great, great grandmother Marta, the wife of Ante Plosnic, who was born in Stobrec circa 1800, as Don Branko Stepinac told me at our earlier interview, and as Matko now confirms. Matko then tells me that he himself was born and raised in the house right next door to my grandmother's home, and that the two houses are separated by a distance of only one meter. Matko could have been my childhood playmate.

Matko spreads across the table several old black and white photographs of the Vusic house. World War II was not kind to the place. One photograph shows it occupied by a dozen Italian soldiers in gray uniforms. After Italy's defeat, Nazi troops moved into Stobrec and used my grandmother's birthplace as a prison for Polish soldiers. In 1945, after Germany's surrender, several mines stored in the house exploded and destroyed it. As a young boy, Matko remembers the Vusic house, the birthplace of my grandmother and their family home since 1800, as "a ghost house without a roof." My questions about the difficulty of life in Croatia during World War II are answered by these photographs of Italian soldiers on parade in Stobrec and the history of our family home. The Vusic house is now owned by non-Dalmatians who purchased it in the 1970's, renovated it in an unattractive style, illegally added a third-story apartment, covered the original white stone walls with a stucco finish which they painted orange, and who are still perceived today as big time interlopers, outsiders, and gate crashers because they have lived in Stobrec for only thirty-five years or so and because they bastardized a village gem. No one in Stobrec so much as nods to them, an unfortunate aspect of tight-woven neighborhood life, where everyone knows your business and have forgotten nothing. Little Stobrec, like the Balkans, can be a village of long remembered offenses.

This house is located on Mornarska Street, the street of the Plosnics and the lifeblood of Stobrec, thirty meters below Tatiana's home and the restaurant Epetium. It is the only house on the ancient street turned on its axis, breaking up the tidy row. The house is built on a rocky sea cliff, literally on top of the sea. It is no great wonder I feel the Adriatic in my bones. The stories my mother told me about the house were all true. In winter, heavy storms brought high waves from the Adriatic crashing against the rocks, showering its front door with sea spray.

Whereas Branko Stepinac presented my family line in outline form, Matko has produced an almost entirely complete version extending back to the birth of Ante, with the birth years, years of death, the names of spouses, and the names and number of their children. My people had large families; my grandmother was one of eight; her father was one of six. They were also long-lived. Even during the mid-1800's, they were living into their 70's and 80's. There are also notations on the family tree about my grandmother and her siblings. "Left for America" is the notation for three of them. One of her sisters, Lucia, had two notations: "Left for America," and "Died in Italy." Lucia, it may be assumed, did not like America, and returned to die in Europe, or perhaps she left for America, only to make it as far as Italy. She lived to age 72. Tereza's notation is "died unmarried." "Left for America" has a hollow sadness to it, seen within the context of this small reunion in the wooded hills above Split.

Then Matko shifts gears and presents another document, this one a history of the family origins in Stobrec. Tatiana has seen this before and is waving it off, saying "no, no."

According to this research, compiled over a period of years and written by Matko, who is now finishing a second volume of Stobrec history, the very first of our relatives to appear in the village were two brothers, Ivan and Iliya, who arrived with their families in 1659. All Plosnics in Stobrec, whether they like each other or not, are descended from one of these two brothers.

Tatiana bridles at this version of events. She believes we are descended from Ivan and Iliya, but that we go back at least four hundred years earlier.

Matko the historian says yes, perhaps, but he has yet to find solid evidence to support that claim.

"The brothers Ivan and Iliya are the founders of our family, in the mid-seventeenth century," Matko states. "All of us originate from one of them or the other. We do not know how they arrived in Stobrec, and none of us alive knows which of the two brothers is our direct ancestor. The best we can say is that we are descended from one of them. They are the Romulus and Remus of our family tree." Konstantin, smiling, looks satisfied with Matko's version.

"There is an excellent reason Tatiana so closely resembles your mother, as you say," Matko says to me. "She is your blood relative."

Then, slowly and dramatically, Matko extends his deeply tanned right arm and points his index finger around the table to Tatiana, Konstantin, and the Big Fixer, and then he pats himself on the heart, fixing me with a look and says: "You see, we are your family. We are far from perfect—and you would err to romanticize us too much—but we belong to each other, and we will be part of each other's lives forever."

We all nod, grinning warmly at each other around the table. For the first time today, no one has anything to say.

Konstantin then stands and takes me in his arms.

"Thank you for finding us," he says, looking me in the eyes.

"Thank you for taking me in," I tell him.

———⇒•⇐———

This is the last I would see of Tatiana—at least in 2008— my cousin from the Adriatic, a woman from a traditional Dalmatian family with three children and a sweet-natured husband, who I love as powerfully as the suppressed and forgotten love of my mother.

"What can I do for you?" I ask in the flurry of our goodbyes, holding her by the arms. I know there is nothing I can do and that she will ask nothing of me.

Immediately, she looks as if she has formulated a reply. She is unsurprised by my question and has something specific in mind, but she quickly catches herself and pulls back.

"You never know," she says with her smile and that shrug of hers. Is she thinking about her children, about providing them shelter in America in the event of another war in Croatia, or is it about money, as Dorothy might surmise? Whatever the request, my answer is yes.

"I love you, Tatiana, and I love your father and your family. I thank you for everything you have done. You will never know how much you mean to me. You have made me feel that Split is my home, my city. You bring it all alive for me."

She is so lovely it pains me to look at her. All day I was afraid I would embarrass myself or cross lines of demarcation if I gazed at her because I wanted to study her for clues to my history and not look away. Throughout the day I yearned to connect with her but did not know if such an effort would be wrong, or inappropriate, or offensive to Vlado, so I just sat back enviously watching her old uninhibited friend Dundo hug and flirt with her.

Tatiana has gone to some length to make herself especially pretty for this celebration on the Marjan. She's wearing beige trousers with a white blouse and beige sweater, all very flattering, an ensemble that might have come from Banana Republic. It still shocks me to see her in modern garb, as if expecting her to wear the black shroud of Paulina Plosnic, circa 1910, or dressed in the mode preferred by my mother in the 1970's. Her hair and make-up have been given extra care today. Her lipstick, in my mother's favorite deep-red hue, was applied just so. She sat beside me at the big banquet table throughout the day, her fine scent and sweet breath upon me, but I was reluctant to turn my head in her direction or touch her hand.

Tatiana takes a breath and says to me with a smile: "I feel like I have always known you, that you have always been a part of my life." I not could imagine a deeper acknowledgment or more perfect goodbye.

"And yes. There is something you can do for me," she says with that tilt of her head, looking into my eyes. "Don't forget us. And promise that you will return."

Seven

ONE GOOD THING

Croatia Airlines is not on the scale of United or Lufthansa but it surpasses the membership requirements for Croatia's entry into the European Union. It operates a fleet of just ten aircraft, four sparkling white A319's, four brand-new A320's, and two fuel-efficient Dash-8's, with the red and white colors of the Croatian flag proudly displayed on their tails, and all piloted by captains who flew combat missions during the Yugoslavia War. After purchasing a bottle of Dalmatian olive oil in the Duty Free shop, I head over to my flight, which departs Split on an exquisite blue morning precisely on time, and gets into cold and foggy Munich where Nat, who has just arrived from San Francisco, meets me with a warm, weary smile at the gate and drives me to his apartment on Rupprechstrasse in good old Mr. Bluey, where we both take a much needed nap. Later that evening, Nat, his wonderful fiance Stephanie, and I go to Café Neuhausen for dinner, my favorite restaurant in their elegant neighborhood, within walking distance of their top-floor apartment. I love going to Café Neuhausen for my Munich fix of schnitzel and Lowenbrau hefeweizen, brewed just down the street at the block-long brewery on Nymphenburgerstrasse. Nat and Stephanie discuss their wedding plans. They hope to be married in Italy, next fall, which means, I am thinking to myself, that I will be back in Dalmatia by then, at the latest. Octoberfest is in full swing in Munich, and the city is full of loud public drunks staggering around the city streets, watched like hawks by edgy-looking clusters of police officers in immaculate white rain coats, ready to make arrests. Early the next morning, just before sunrise, I say goodbye to Nat and Stephanie, take a taxi back to the gorgeous Munich airport, and board the nine-hour Lufthansa flight westward to Washington.

My reliable burgundy-colored SUV, washed over by weeks of rain and speckled with mud, abandoned where I left it in a far corner of a distant satellite parking lot at Dulles airport, roars back to life with the first turn of the key, but even so, it still costs nearly $400 to extricate. My cell phone, which I had left turned off in the driver's side door pocket, springs back too, so after I pay and head out onto Route 28, I immediately call my brother, at his desk in his law office, who gives me his somber but steady take on recent U.S. events. Then I call the Big Firm and speak with William, the fine young man who received my client accounts, and fortunately he is still at work and still sounds upbeat about life. I don't ask about anyone in the office, but he volunteers that three other brokers, Meshuggina, Fatboy Slim, and The Ancient Mariner, have left, three more names to be added to The List. Wait. Stop. I am done with The List. The last name to appear on The List was my own.

Travel is about the departure and the return. Most of the time when one arrives home the place looks exceptional. Coming back, even after a few days, brings the pleasure of rediscovering beloved territory. On this occasion, however, it would not.

I'm driving back home to a shit storm. All the terrible news I successfully deflected during September in far-off Dalmatia will now strike me with full force. Some think I have abandoned them, some don't understand what I am doing, most are completely uninterested in my level of emotional fulfillment. With the stock market crash and now the looming fear of total collapse, everyone is searching for a plan, shelter from the storm, or someone to blame.

Heading home from the airport, taking the route I have driven hundreds of times between Dulles and Charlottesville, I somehow get lost and drive thirty miles out of my way far off to the west on Route 66 before realizing I am going in the wrong direction. Maybe I don't want to be going home. I never understood why my grandmother left Stobrec in 1913, and I don't understand why I am returning to Charlottesville today, except that Charlottesville is home, and that home is the place where, when you go there, they have to take you in. Now, behind the wheel, for the first time in months, I am quavering and short of breath, bracing myself, anticipating physical assault. I am about to see my old familiar world through a Dalmatian lens and I am afraid how it's going to appear.

As I finally enter the city limits on Route 29, I decide to make a quick stop at Whole Foods. Maybe I'll pick up some fruit, I don't know what I am thinking. But I am not inside my local Whole Foods store more than a minute when I see Ashley Carrington near the cheese counter, a talented pianist, multimillionaire, always elegantly attired. She pushes her overflowing grocery cart of Whole Food delicacies directly at me with eyes wide, blocking my path, and demands: "Are you afraid?"

My suitcases are still in the car. It is starting already.

"Afraid of what?"

"I don't want to be poor."

She and her husband live in one of the great country estates of Albemarle County, a nineteenth century horse farm with outbuildings, cottages, and splendid views of the Blue Ridge Mountains.

"No, I am not afraid," I sputter. "And you will never be poor."

The magnificent displays in Whole Foods exceeds even the abundance of the garden in the Marjan, but the mood here is far from festive.

Not a minute later, in the dairy aisle, I am spotted by Megan Court, a real-estate agent, who immediately asks me, with furrowed brow: "Are you worried?" She does not say hello; she does not ask after my well-being. She just asks if I am worried. She looks fragile, physically unwell. The sudden change in her appearance alarms me. She has lost twenty pounds since I saw her last.

"Worried about what?" I know precisely what she is talking about.

She speed recites a panoply of pain, all the headlines from CNN. Fear in the Whole Foods.

"No, I am not worried," I tell her, looking into her eyes. "We are going to get through this, I promise you. Please try not to worry."

My response seems to momentarily calm her. She allows a tight smile to form in the corners of her mouth. She has finally met someone who is not worried. Everyone needs reassurance. They are all in a panic. I can't get out of Whole Foods fast enough. Another woman, the wife of a successful developer, tries to flag me down in the parking lot descending from her silver Lexus. I wave at her as I race back to my car. This is my hometown. I am back on the Riva. I know virtually everyone. My game plan, to avoid toxic people, is not going to work here.

I want to tell them that a sudden fall in the value of their portfolio from all-time highs is painful, not apocalyptic, that their safety is not at risk, that invading troops are not massing on the border, but I can't think on my feet fast enough. I've got jet lag; I did not anticipate this onslaught; their fear and agitation are overwhelming obstacles. It is as if they believe, by acting fearfully, they can vanquish the fear-making event. It is already obvious that what I learned in Split will be trivial to them. I am hoping that what I learned will be sufficient to get me through the crisis.

My wife isn't home when I walk in the kitchen door even though she knows the day and hour of my arrival. She comes in only after I have unpacked, run two loads of laundry, and showered, slightly irritated with me for not remembering her schedule. "I had a meeting. I told you," she says.

There is no Adriatic Sea in Charlottesville but there are plenty of drowning people. No one is glad to see me, but no one looks happy to see anyone. No one looks happy, period. Charlottesville is grim, like the seating area outside the emergency room. I look around for carefree smiling faces and don't see any. The only people who are acting naturally are the belligerent public drunks on the Downtown Mall. Many look pale and vulnerable, like the rug has been pulled out from under them. I see—and will continue to see—a lot of people working hard to keep up appearances, but the strain is showing. It is October 1, 2008.

I have received a long, rambling, faintly hostile email message from one of my oldest friends, essentially accusing me of deserting him during his hour of need, and I agree to meet him for coffee at Shenandoah Joe's, as lively as a funeral parlor. Email is a dangerous medium. It's far too easy to write what you really think late at night, under the influence, the sedatives just kicking in, and hit "send."

Henry is experienced, hardworking, an advisor to many. He and his wife were among the guests at the C&O for my Big Firm farewell party. Now he is perspiring and flipped out. I am shocked to see him in such obvious distress.

"I was in total panic," he tells me as we sit down, passing across to me a handwritten, worried-over list of all the stocks and mutual funds he sold as the market started its nose-dive. "I was in a real cycle—wine in the evening, Ambien to fall sleep, wide awake at 3 A.M., watching the Asian markets on my computer, getting up early, making a pot of coffee, and watching 'Squawk Box' on CNBC. And those Virginia municipal bonds you sold me? Thanks! They cratered."

Oy vey.

This exact scenario, this death march, this cycle of disabling fear, was worlds away when I was gone. I take a deep breath. All I am trying to do now is to stay calm and protect myself.

Then he looks at me askance, as if I were an insect, and says: "What are you doing?"

As if I should be down the hole with him.

I have trouble responding to his question. I have no big sales figure to report. I try to tell him about the trip just completed, about my happy transition, about lessons learned on the Dalmatian coast, but he is not listening or has no interest.

"I'm going to write a book about it," I tell him. I don't know why I volunteer this information.

This comment captures his fractured attention.

"A book? Are you nuts? No one buys books anymore. No one reads. Kindle is putting books out of business." This is his quick, back-of-the-envelope market analysis.

Then suddenly he turns cruel.

"You know, you really ought to get a job or rent an office somewhere before your wife throws you out of the house," my old friend of twenty years tells me. "I ran into her downtown when you were gone. She said she was so busy with work she was sort of glad you weren't there."

Precisely as he intends, his words sting. He had been rehearsing this speech until the day he saw me, and now he's fired off both barrels. Right there at Shenandoah Joe's, a long relationship takes a turn in a new direction.

The next day, I have errands to run. At Sam's Club, all the prices are marked clearly and no one attempts to rip you off. Good. The only problem is, I have to buy sixty four rolls of toilet paper and twenty four replacement blades for my Gillette Fusion razor.

As I wander around this big concrete warehouse, someone gently taps me on the shoulder. It's a Sam's Club employee wearing a Yankees cap and an oversized, red circus clown vest, with a giant name tag attached to his chest that reads: "Hi, My Name is Chief."

The guy behind the red vest and name badge is indeed the Chief, the one and only, the so-called Grand Fromage, my former boss at the Big Firm, now employed by Sam's Club. He tries to give me a big hug.

"What are you staring at?" the Grand Fromage asks me, laughing.

I am staring at him, slack-jawed, dumbfounded. This guy was a multimillion dollar producer, a *boulevardier* who wore handmade pinstripe suits and John Lobb shoes. One day, he just lost his mojo and quit.

"What are you doing here?" I ask him.

"I'm a cashier."

Holy shit, mother fucking....

But the Grand Fromage is completely at ease, standing under the fluorescent lights of Sam's, smiling and laughing out loud, a ray of sunshine. At least one person appears healthy and unfazed by the madness in the streets. When he offers his confident, stay-the-course stock market advice, I am aware that I am carefully attending the economic outlook, as good as anyone's, of a cashier at Sam's Club.

A couple of mornings later I am back at Shenandoah Joe's for the great coffee and run into Sergeant Bilko, another name from The List, one of the University of Virginia graduates who could not cut the mustard at the Big Firm and quit or was fired within a year of his start date. He still has a flat top but has grown a thick black goatee since I saw him last. Bilko is a young man, in his early 30's, with a wife and child. Hanging out at Shenandoah Joe's on a Friday morning in jeans and a goatee probably means Bilko is successfully maintaining his self-employed status. Sitting down with him, he makes polite conversation for a minute or two and then asks me, with a troubled expression on his brow, for advice about his career. Touched by his sincerity, I tell him he should get out of financial services, that selling securities is no career at all, that he is young and that now is a good time to discover who he is and what he truly loves to do. The upside to the downside, I try to tell him, is the chance to examine his life with care, but I am absolutely certain he does not hear me.

In the Most Happy Nations table just published, the United States ranks 23rd of all countries in happiness, which strikes me as generous. Denmark is number one, according to the BBC, where personal freedom is more important than money. Pew Research publishes a poll: "Half of all Americans would rather live somewhere else." Another study says that happiness spreads like a contagion, as does fear. The happiness study suggests that it is one's duty, if you have a friend who is negative and fearful, not to drop that person from your roster of friends, but to spread happiness to him. The study suggests laughter, too, is contagious. Someone should go into Shenandoah Joe's and just start laughing.

My conservative chums are increasingly agitated as the election nears and an Obama victory appears likely. Obama gives me hope for America's revival, a new start for me and for the country I love. Their rants are exhausting. The malevolence of the political season has sliced and diced even my closest friendships.

This is my beloved home, preferable to Chicago for me because it was small and comprehensible, and because it saved my life when I first moved here. But the town has grown threefold, and while still a buffer, it has lost its innocence and immunity. If I am going to live here with health and happiness, I am going to need a modest recipe and a continued boycott of the 24/7 news cycle. The only important item I missed during my self-imposed embargo was the breakup of Levi Johnston and Bristol Palin.

Perhaps the Bloomfield Road Bicycle Club will be my community this year. At least it's a start.

Finding community, as I learned in Dalmatia, is essential, and we find it in very small places. My neighborhood association plants trees every couple of years. That's a small community effort. Buying Girl Scout cookies from a neighborhood Girl Scout who comes to your door is a basic minimum requirement for being in community, if you like Girl Scout cookies or not.

Knowing where I come from helps me know who I am and stay focused on the moment. One can never have too much self-knowledge. Without guidance, even smart and seasoned people get lost. I come from a small peninsula on the Adriatic Sea. Please, America, I am a person of simple Mediterranean origin, a village of just 3,000. Don't make it too complicated for me.

A week after my return to the United States I am atop the Cumberland plateau in middle Tennessee attending parent weekend at The University of the South. I feel grounded and connected with my youngest daughter and her world. Then, I organize a trip back to California to grab my infant granddaughter to share my philosophy of life, and tell her about her great, great, great, great, grandmother's stone birthplace above the Adriatic, and how unwanted interlopers, out and out newcomers to our ancestral village, have totally screwed up its renovation.

The Piedmont Virginia winter passes, cold and rainy and bleak. The town feels abandoned. Even the street people have disappeared from the Downtown Mall. The times are not easy. All the experts are wrong about everything. There is a big shake out going on. When change comes, it comes hard. I see people clinging, clinging, clinging to their old ways, in their old clothes and dusty offices, hoping when the bounce back comes, their old lives will bounce back too, exactly as they were before. They think they need to just get through it.

In the midst of this, I make a trip back to Chicago, my first in a decade, to attend my high school reunion and to see my Aunt Dorothy, now past her 90th birthday, and bring with me several hundred photographs of Tatiana, Konstantin, Split, Stobrec, and the Vusic house, birthplace of her mother. Dorothy urged me to make the journey to Dalmatia. Without Paulina's birth certificate, which Dorothy sent, the connection to my cousins and their village would have been more difficult to prove. I owed it to Dorothy to make this visit before she died. A phone call to her in the nursing home would not suffice.

After landing at O'Hare, I drive the rental car to her big austere building on grimy Southport Avenue, and immediately, upon entering the lobby, my gag reflex kicks in, set off by the standard nursing home fragrance of urine commingled with strong cleansing agent. I cannot help but juxtapose the life of the aged women of Stobrec, congregating on starry evenings on their stone benches on Mornarska Street, with these old ladies on Southport Avenue, sequestered inside their units.

But Dorothy looks robust, and she still has that tough old Chicago attitude. She has a full head of gray and brown hair, and sits upright in her armchair. Her sixth floor apartment surprises me with its spaciousness. It is spotless, attractively furnished, and has a great southerly view towards the Loop. I stay for hours, much longer than I had planned. Dorothy takes me to lunch in the restaurant downstairs, proudly leading me around, introducing me to all the old women at adjacent tables. It is a pleasure to see the authentic compassion of the staff—black, white, and hispanic—looking after the elderly black, white, and hispanic residents. Chicago is rainbow hued, suddenly alive and desirable to me.

Dorothy never married. Thanks to her malicious wit and acid tongue, she alienated her mother, my mother, her brothers, her one lovely niece, and her nephews. When she tells me I am the first person to visit in all her years in the nursing home I am saddened but not surprised. She looks at me in wonder, like an apparition. She asks me—twenty times—to identify myself. She clings to me. She does not want me to leave. The first picture I show her is a photograph of Tatiana in profile, sitting in the sunshine of a Dalmatian morning in that café on the Riva. When Dorothy sees it she intones immediately and as a matter-of-fact: "that's Goldie." Her sister, my beautiful mother.

"I was the smart one in the family," Dorothy tells me. "Your mother was the great beauty."

That evening, at the big New Trier reunion at Hackney's on Lake Street, three hundred former classmates gather, at least half of them, like me, starting over, with nervous smiles on their faces, hoping for new connections with old friends. I relax among them, and do not feel alone.

The next morning I drive far south across the city to St. Jerome's Croatian Catholic Church on Princeton Avenue, the old neighborhood, as my parents called it, for an appointment with the priest, Jozo Grbes, with whom I have been corresponding by email. St. Jerome's is the church where my immigrant grandparents were married and where my mother and her siblings were baptized and educated. We are one of the founding families of St. Jerome's. Father Joe greets me warmly in the church office by saying: "You have been on a long journey—from the unknown to the known."

Father Joe tells me that when he returns to Croatia to see family and friends, they tell him "welcome home," and that when he returns to Chicago from Croatia his friends and church community welcome him back with the same expression. He shakes his head with a smile. He understands bifurcation and divided loyalties. He also says that a church fails an individual at "the point of rejection," and he believes that life is empty without any deep spiritual connection. He tells me that the Jewish and Catholic faiths are intertwined, based on the same liturgy, and that, in his view, a mixed Jewish-Catholic ancestry is "a beautiful complement." I never considered this. To say that I am grateful to him is an understatement. Father Joe has opened my mind.

When I leave him, I drive up the street a few blocks to 2606 Princeton Avenue, my mother's birthplace, according to her birth certificate held in the well-organized archives at St. Jerome's. The house at 2606 no longer exists. In its place is one of the massive concrete pillars supporting the Stevenson Expressway high overhead.

Father Joe showed me in the church ledger that my mother was born July 3, 1921, and was christened Amalia Ljubica: Amalia, the Latin for Goldie; Ljubica, Croatian for Violet. Goldie Violet Plosnic Simundza Friedman. Ronnie, to her husband and friends.

Home again, as if for the first time.

Now, the production of one well-crafted object is my daily prayer. Give me, I pray of you, one good thing to do well. Allow me entry to that process and by chance the joy of the new morning. Help make my life simple and comprehensible, as it once was, when I was a boy. With the black and silver crucifix of my grandmother Paulina Plosnic worn round my neck, I pray this of you.

My spit sample has been analyzed by 23andme and my DNA results returned. The Y chromosome of my paternal origin suggests that the worlds of Sephardim and Ashkenazi are not so distinct or clear cut in my case, even though my father's mother spoke Yiddish and looked like Golda Meir. We may have found ourselves in the Pale of Settlement in the nineteenth century, in present day Belarus, but we arrived there from Turkey and I have not a drop of northern blood in me. Ethiopian Jews, Jordanian men who live along the Dead Sea, the Jews of Libya, Sicilians, Sardinians, Palestinians, Syrians, peoples of the Levant, the Holy Land, the eastern Mediterranean, these are who I am and where I come from via my old man. On my mother's side, my mitochondrial DNA is a rifle shot to a small stone village on the Adriatic Sea. By heredity, I should not live in a landlocked locale. I should own a boat. I should be drinking wine and eating olives every day.

It is very early spring, not the single smallest bud has appeared in the mountain wilderness of Tennessee, the Sewanee Division III women's lacrosse team is set to open play against Bates College on a bitterly cold afternoon, and as difficult as it is to get to Sewanee from Charlottesville, I vow to attend as many games as I can, with my brown-eyed baby daughter a star on the field and wanting me there for her to call for her and cheer her name. Seeing her run—from earliest childhood, fearless, gifted with great speed—and now watching her race up the field, lifts my heart and inspires me with hope. And then, after the important triumph over Denison in mid-March, a come-from-behind victory by a single goal, the biggest win of this promising new season, the athletes, the coaches, and the parents all come together and celebrate a moment of pure joy, slapping each other on the back, clearing our lungs singing their praises to the cold Tennessee sky. We are a unit. Our beautiful daughters played with exceptional skill and heart, and we love being together like this, to raise them up and hold them in our arms with pride. There's an intoxicating rumor working its way through the team and its small but passionate band of followers, that if we get just one or two more victories this season, the Tigers of the University of the South might be bound for the NCAA tournament. That is an event I do not intend to miss.

Appendix for Travelers

SPLIT

Places to eat....

Restaurant Epetium
3 Mornarska, Stobrec, 21311
Tel. 385-21-324-126
Email: epetium@st.t-com.hr
My family's restaurant (since 1967) on the ancient peninsula in the village of Stobrec, a fifteen minute cab ride from central Split. Open only at dinner. The best seafood in Dalmatia.

Picaferaj
Popovica 2, Split.
Tel. 385-91-517-6868
Located in the picturesque Veli Varos neighborhood, my favorite "hole in the wall" in Split. Be sure to ask for Ivo.

Nostromo
10 Krag Svete Marije, Split
Tel. 385-91-405-6666
An elegant restaurant with fine service and outstanding selection of Dalmatian wines located across the alley from the Split fish market featuring fresh seafood from the Adriatic.

There are many traditional taverns in Split and across Dalmatia called *Kanoba*, which can be wonderful for lunch and dinner. Especially recommended are **Kanoba Varos** (Split, Ban Miadenova 7; Tel. 385-21-396-138); **Sperun** (Split, Sperun 3; Tel. 385-21-346-999); and a local favorite, the atmospheric **Ostarija Vidakovi** near Bacvice Beach and the Hotel Park (Tel. 385-21-489-106).

Places to stay....

The **Hotel Vestibule Palace** is the most elegant (and costly) hotel in central Split. It features a magnificent, private location in a quiet corner of Diocletian's Palace, refined service, and an excellent restaurant.
www.vestibulpalace.com

The **Hotel Slavija** is another attractive hotel option inside the walls of Diocletian's Palace, if a notch or two in quality below the Vestibule Palace. Small guest rooms, no elevator.
www.hotelslavija.com

The **Hotel Park** is the sentimental choice with its exquisite location on Bacvice Beach, but its guest rooms are small, dark, and in dire need of refurbishment.
www.hotelpark-split.hr.com

Dundo's romantic retreat in the beautiful mountain hinterland above Split—the **Villa Olka**—has just been opened as a five-room hotel with diversions ranging from hunting to winemaking. See *www.villa-olka.com* for details.

Email: info@villa-olka.com
Tel. 385-98-222-509

Places to see....

Split's public beaches at Bacvice, Firule, and on the Marjan, are among the most beautiful in the Mediterranean region. They are all within a fifteen minute walk of central Split.

Public ferries depart from the port of Split everyday to the islands of Brac, Hvar, and Korcula. Buses are available every hour in high-season from Split to Trogir and several times daily from Split to Dubrovnik.

The Ivan Mestrovic Museum & Gardens is located along the sea on the Marjan, about a twenty-five minute walk from the Riva. During the high season it is open Tuesday-Sunday from 10:00 AM until 6:30 PM (closed Monday).

Informative Links....

Apartments or houses available for rent in Split or on the islands, and yacht charters (bareboat or with crew), can be found on any number of sites, including: *www.dalmacija.net*

Selected Bibliography

Ivo Andric: *The Bridge on the Drina*, translated by Lovett F. Edwards (University of Chicago Press, 1977).

Saul Bellow: *The Advenures of Augie March* (Weidenfeld & Nicholson, 1954).

Lawrence Durrell: *Justine* (E.P. Dutton, 1957).

Lawrence Durrell: *Prospero's Cell* (E.P. Dutton & Co., 1960).

Robert Frost: "The Death of the Hired Man," (1915).

Hugh Johnson and Jancis Robinson: *The World Atlas of Wine* (Mitchell Beazley, 2007).

Robert D. Kaplan: *Balkan Ghosts: A Journey Through History* (Picador, 2005).

Andrew Marvell: "The Garden," *The New Oxford Book of English Verse, 1250-1950,* edited by Helen Gardner (Oxford University Press, 1972).

Wallace Stevens: "The Anecdote of the Jar," *The Collected Works of Wallace Stevens,* (Knopf, 1970).

Rebecca West: *Black Lamb and Grey Falcon*, introduction by Christopher Hitchens (Penguin Books, 2007).

Acknowledgements

I acknowledge my love for and the profound assistance of:

Nat Friedman, who led me to Dalmatia; Peach Friedman, for copyediting the manuscript and setting the standard for our family in the arena of memoir; and Victoria Friedman, my beautiful Southern daughter and genius on the field of life, for her insights as I wrote this book.

The entire Plosnic family of Stobrec, Dalmatia, for their open hearts, their kindness and hospitality. May God protect you and keep you safe.

Paulina and Zelimir Vidjak, and their children and grandchildren Marina, Sandra, Ivan, Rino and Luka.

Dundo Zelimir Dundic, the abiding spirit of the mountains and the sea, gifted host, musician, and human being.

Bruna Reic, former concierge of the Hotel Park, now concierge of the Atrium Hotel, Split, without whose effort this story would never have unfolded.

Father Jozo Grbes of St. Jerome's Croatian Catholic Church of Chicago, for his history lessons, generosity, and deep commitment to the community he serves.

Alijana Vuksic of the Croatian National Tourism Board, Stobrec.

Nevena Cikes of the Hotel Park, Split, Croatia.

The staff of the Croatian Embassy, Washington, DC.

Dr. Jeffrey Fracher of Charlottesville for helping me get started.

Stephen J. McNaughton for critical support during an important life transition.

Cathie Brettschneider of the University of Virginia Press for her encouragement along the way.

Browning Porter for his beautiful graphic design.

And Bob, Bruce, Joe, Tom, and Tony, for all the years of friendship, talk, and real community.

Breinigsville, PA USA
31 March 2011
258853BV00001B/2/P